Indianapolis Roadsters

1952–1964

Joe Scalzo

MOTORBOOKS

First published in 1999 by Motorbooks, an imprint of MBI Publishing Company, Galtier Plaza, Suite 200, 380 Jackson Street, St. Paul, MN 55101-3885 USA

Motorbooks titles are also available at discounts in bulk quantity for industrial or sales-promotional use. For details write to Special Sales Manager at MBI Publishing Company, Galtier Plaza, Suite 200, 380 Jackson Street, St. Paul, MN 55101-3885 USA.

ISBN 0-7603-0634-6

Edited by Kris Palmer
Designed by Rebecca Allen

Printed in China

On the front cover: Rodger Ward powers his way to the win at 1962's Indianapolis 500. *Bob Tronolone*

On the frontispiece: A. J. Watson (center) and his roadster-building troop were at the top of America's racing game when this photo was snapped in 1956. All were immensely talented, independent, and driven to win. Hank Blum (left) works on a championship dirt car and Jim Flaherty assists Watson. *Lester Nehamkin, Mike Flaherty collection*

On the title page: All 11 rows on the pace lap for the 1962 Indy 500. *Bob Tronolone*

On the back cover: Top: Dick Rathmann at the wheel of the McNamara Motor Freight in 1958. This car managed five consecutive Indy starts, setting a speed record in 1958, before finally retiring after the 1962 race. *Indy 500 photo* **Bottom:** Dart Kart 83, piloted by rookie Donnie Davis, looked great before it blew oil all over its tires then slid and spun its way down the front straightaway. *Bob Tronolone*

CONTENTS

INDIANAPOLIS, CALIFORNIA

Before racing had so much money, technology, and safety, there used to be a Tyrannosaurus Rex of race cars. Few may remember these extinct reptiles, but the Hall of Fame Museum at the Indianapolis Motor Speedway keeps some on display. And if after looking at them in the museum you felt the need to see a whole pack of them together in anger, you used to be able to head over to the ground floor of the Speedway's Tower Terrace Section and confront a tinted, oversized photograph hanging there.

It was the start of the 38th running of the 500-mile race, May 30, 1956. The front row of three big speedway-type single-seaters with long hoods, dropped noses, and tall, thin tires were careening across the white starting strip and you could almost hear the damn things running. On the outside, close to the grandstands, the Ansted Rotary, a Kurtis-Kraft, was ahead of the middle automobile, the Lindsey Hopkins, another Kurtis-Kraft. Off on the inside right, the John Zink No. 8, a white-and-pink Watson, was falling back. Whamming away at each other close behind came 26 almost identical monsters.

They were known as Meyer-Drake Offenhauser roadsters, Offy roadsters, championship roadsters, Indy-type roadsters, big cucumbers, and dinosaurs. It took a four-spoke steering wheel to aim and control one, plus two dampers per wheel, eight in all, to shock one, and something like 30 pounds of high-test aviation nuts and bolts and safety wire to tie one together. Counting the skeleton of chrome molybdenum steel and ancillary armament, plus its hogshead of racing fuel and its driver, a roadster might go fully loaded at better than a dead-weight ton. Almost 500 pounds of that tonnage was engine, the barrel-type crankcase, Meyer-Drake Offenhauser four-cylinder. A hammering mass of drumming pistons, whirring connecting rods, throbbing crankshaft, and sobbing Hilborn fuel injection, an Offy got a roadster going faster and faster along Indy's 3/4-mile straightaways until the speed topped out at above 170 miles per hour. It was a great antique and a violent shaker, the Offy. People still talk about its roaring, runaway sound.

Above Dinosaurs under the Hoosier sun. Gasoline Alley, May 1963. *Bob Tronolone*

Opposite page: *Mike Flaherty collection*

Every successful roadster used the Offy, but there was radical disagreement about where in the engine bay to put it and about what would make a roadster go fastest without wearing out tires in the 800 left-hand turns of the Indy 500. Some roadsters seated their drivers to the left with the Offenhauser and its madly revolving drive shaft on the right; others did exactly the opposite. At least one fast and maverick roadster had its Offy angled diagonally from left front to right rear. Operating on the theory of reducing roadster wind resistance, and dropping the center of gravity, certain Offenhausers wound up laying almost flat on their sides, fuel-injection horns booming up through the top of the hood.

But whether it was a reverse-weight Kurtis-Kraft, or a Kuzma, Lesovsky, or Epperly lowbelly laydown, or a Watson upright with its flaring shark nose, watching such vehicles race was an amazing experience. In fact, anybody who ever saw the coachworks of cold-rolled aluminum, bright in the sticky humidity of Memorial Day Indiana—the flanks plastered with decals from Perfect Circle Piston Rings, Bear Wheel Alignment, Champion and Autolite Spark Plugs, Raybestos brake linings, Monroe and Premier shock absorbers, Bowes Seal Fast, and the flying red Pegasus of Mobil Petroleum, the big-armed driver wearing tanker goggles and the roadster's colossal 8:00x18 Firestone tires standing as high as his helmet—anybody who ever witnessed all that, or ever heard a big roadster at full revs running loose around the top of the Speedway, understands why the roadster in its heyday was the symbol of Indianapolis, and the greatest of all American race cars to see in combat or merely standing still.

Once roadsters were commonplace. Oval track racing cultist and historian Bob Mount estimates that during the roadster era, roughly 1952 through 1964, some 103 roadsters were racing at Indy. And if you are wondering how it came to be that these race cars, which won 12 of 13 500s, a dozen in succession, originated not in Indianapolis itself, but half a continent away in Los Angeles, California, you can, in effect, credit World War II. L.A., after all, was

Its boomy Meyer-Drake Offenhauser and primitive bucket seat were bolted directly to its chassis. Its Firestone tires were hard as rocks. And its eight very stiff shock absorbers passed along every bump in the Brickyard. Driving a dinosaur roadster was like hanging onto a piece of machinery that was trying to jump out of its skin. Most times, a brave driver who jabbed away at the throttle and battled the four-spoke steering wheel could keep his car in the race. But not always. The Hoover Motor Express, an Epperly lowbelly laydown, walled itself in 115 miles on Memorial Day 1963. *Bob Tronolone*

accessories for roadster teams such as Agajanian Willard Battery, Dean Van Lines, Vita Fresh Orange Juice, Bowes Seal Fast, and Sheraton-Thompson.

Master bodyman, welder, aluminum beater, "Eddie Ka-Zoom" had been an L.A. fixture since the war. He made lots of money but seldom spent it, and for this and other peculiarities he was regarded as the closest thing to an artist that L.A. racing society boasted. And at times, an eccentric artist at that. One of Eddie's stranger practices was to work with the radio screaming full blast—playing music, the news, whatever—to discourage idle conversation. Once a customer told Eddie what he needed, and Eddie understood, all yakking was concluded and it was time to beat it. Anybody not grasping this did so at their own peril and was liable to get the bum's rush.

All the various Kuzma midgets, sprints, and in particular the almost unbeatable Kuzma dirt championship cars, were revered for their looks and exquisite and detailed finishes. Kuzma's roadsters were less highly regarded, although his Greenman-Casale of 1957, with its Maserati Formula One lines, was a beautifully proportioned dinosaur. Yet only one Kuzma, the 1957 Race of Two Worlds–winning Dean Van Lines 1, was much of a success. And what was perhaps the fastest Kuzma of all, the Vita Fresh Orange Juice, a 1962 Watson clone that Parnelli Jones was reputed to have liked better than his own Agajanian Willard Battery, went winless.

Nobody every really understood why Eddie Kuzma and his loyal crew of some of the most skilled craftsmen in L.A. never better grasped the roadster formula.

host to Douglas, Lockheed, Northrop, and Vultee, and much of World War II's defense industry, and before and after the armistice roadster kings like A. J. Watson were to learn their craft working in L.A.'s military plants and the aerospace industry. Additionally, the vast inventory of war surplus goods supplied roadster builders with the material for everything from the chassis skeleton to the hound's-tooth cockpit upholstery.

Let's visit the five great L.A. roadster fountainheads of Kuzma, Epperly, Lesovsky, Kurtis-Kraft, and Watson and meet the five masters, and some of their men, whose minds fixated on Indianapolis and its 500 for 365 days a year.

Quin

Not many blocks away from Kuzma's joint, quiet, docile Quin Epperly was laboring away at his own roadster business, plus experiencing his own roadster woes. For reasons beyond his control, most of Quin's career was spent around the wrong car owners, the wrong chief mechanics, and the wrong race drivers. Plus, the

Eddie

Eddie Kuzma's shop was down near the fringes of blue-collar inner Los Angeles. Not solely a race car–construction works, it doubled as an emporium specializing in the crisis work of rehabilitating wrecks at bargain-basement rates as well as fabricating

Eddie Kuzma's crowning glories weren't his Indy roadsters but his unstoppable dirt champ cars—winners of nearly 50 percent of all 100-mile boilers contested between 1954 and 1958. The Dean Van Lines 9, champion of 19 mile-track matches, including eight in a row, was the automobile responsible for the legend of Jimmy Bryan. *Russ Read, Joe Scalzo collection*

Indianapolis fates themselves regularly made sure that Quin never caught a break.

Following apprenticeships in the aviation and defense industries, and race car–building time spent at the facilities of Kurtis-Kraft and Lujie Lesovsky, Epperly in the mid-fifties struck out on his own. George Salih, the shop foreman at Meyer-Drake Offenhauser, and a winning chief mechanic of the 500, asked Quin to make the fuel and oil tanks and bodywork for a flat-engined lowbelly roadster based loosely on the 1952 Cummins Diesel Kurtis-Kraft. It was a huge success. Salih's automobile, the Belond Equa-Flow, subsequently won the 1957 and 1958 500s.

Quin had previously designed and constructed an upright roadster of his own, the Hopkins-Chiropractic, which came in second and fifth in the 1957 and 1958 500s, then won the 1957 Milwaukee 200. Still, Epperly welcomed the lowbelly laydown concept as an improvement and proceeded to spend the rest of the fifties and early sixties creating five of them, all heartbreakers.

The first Epperly laydown, the Jones and Maley 3 of 1958, took fourth in that year's 500, but the following May managed to get upside down during practice. A heroic repair job and a do-or-die time trial on the last qualifying weekend followed, but it sawed its crankshaft in the middle of the run and afterward disappeared.

The second Epperly laydown, also of 1958, was the Demler 99. Aggressive personalities were all the rage of the roadster era, and Norm Demler, a New York apple cider and vinegar tycoon from Niagara Falls, was no exception. He also turned out to be a tyrant and a tightwad. After agreeing to pay Quin $13,000 for a lowbelly for firecracker George Amick, Demler initiated a blizzard of design alteration orders. Slightly wacko over Cadillac's Eldorado model, he had Quin alter the normal Epperly tail and shape it like a Caddy fin. Then

L. (for Ludwig, or "Lujie") A. (for Albert) Lesovsky Race Car Engineering was located at 5275 South Figueroa boulevard. Only five Lujie dinosaurs came out of here in six years, but there was something special and alive about each one. *Ron Lesovsky collection*

Demler confronted Quin with a new agenda about shock absorbers. George Amick got into the act next, hitting up Quin about changing the chassis geometry and raising the torsion bars.

Back at the 500, there was a giant falling out between Demler and his chief mechanic, Rocky Philipp. Somehow their war spilled over to involve Epperly as well. As a result, even though Amick rose to the occasion and earned the team lots of prize money by racing the Demler 99 to second place, Demler proceeded to fire everybody and stiff Quin out of some dough he still owed him.

Quin's third laydown, again raced by Amick, was the Bowes Seal Fast of 1959, which set a record-qualifying lap averaging 176.887 miles per hour around Daytona. Afterward it flew endo on the high banks, and Amick was killed. Rebuilt and raced again and again at Indy under various names, it never finished stronger than sixth.

Quin's next lowbelly, the Hoover Motor Express of 1959, took fourth in that May's 500 and seventh in 1961; it was one of his least-exercised creations. But the fifth Epperly lowbelly, the Detroiter Mobile Homes of 1960, originally constructed for a deadbeat of a Michigan plywood merchant, was the most intriguing and jinxed of all Epperly dinosaurs.

The plywood merchant was so delinquent making his payments that Epperly couldn't wrap up construction until it was too late for the Detroiter Mobile Homes to qualify for the 500. So by the summer of 1960 the vehicle was operating under the unusual custodianship of the sharp but moody chief mechanic Johnnie Pouelsen and Pouelsen's young rookie driver friend, the jalopy derby graduate and bad-ass Parnelli Jones. An amazing situation came out of this.

The Detroiter Mobile Homes showcased all of what Quin believed an Offy roadster should be: low torsion bars, right-side driver compartment, and—in dramatic contrast to, say, a flexing Watson upright—the most rigid chassis and stiffest suspension

---

Opposite, top: Quin Epperly's biggest Indy 500 was that of 1958. It was also the temporary vindication of the lowbelly laydown design. The crash disaster of the opening lap took out four Kurtis-Krafts, a Kuzma, and a pair of Watsons, but George Salih's Belond Equa-Flow and two Quin lowbellys—the Demler 99 and the Jones and Maley—raced safely through. They finished first, second, and fourth. *Indy 500 Photos*

Opposite, bottom: Apple cider merchant and Epperly roadster customer Norm Demler, a difficult man, received good entertainment value from his Demler 99, even though it never won a race. No. 99's one-of-a-kind tail fin represented Quin's acknowledgement of Demler's thing for Cadillac Eldorados. *Bob Tronolone*

combination possible. Vindication was not long in coming. That August, in the Milwaukee 200, getting a monster drive from the novice Jones, the Detroiter Mobile Homes started from the front row, clocked the fastest warm-up time on Sunday morning, led the 200 for 13 miles, and just barely lost.

Afterward, Parnelli and Pouelsen were so enthusiastic that they began putting a deal together to have some of their L.A. friends purchase the Detroiter Mobile Homes from the plywood merchant so that Parnelli could race it in the following year's Indy 500. It was a done deal—almost. But that same winter, during some Firestone tests he was conducting in Indianapolis, Tony Bettenhausen finagled a shakedown ride in the Detroiter Mobile Homes for himself—and went into ecstasy. The great war-horse Bettenhausen had competed in other Epperlys—Tony was the guy who'd gotten the Jones and Maley 3 on its back—but none had felt so perfect as this one. As the story goes, Tony sprinted directly from the Epperly to a Gasoline Alley telephone booth to call his moneybags car owner Lindsey Hopkins. He sharply informed Lindsey that if Lindsey didn't immediately buy him, Tony,

the Detroiter Mobile Homes, that he'd quit and go get a new Indy ride with J. C. Agajanian.

The threat worked. Hopkins purchased the Detroiter Mobile Homes out from under Parnelli and Pouelsen and turned it over to Tony. Still exhilarated by the turn of events, Bettenhausen, while passing through L.A. that January en route to a Honolulu vacation, stopped in at Epperly's to guarantee Quin that the elusive 150-mile-per-hour lap at the Speedway was at long last going to be achieved in 1961, and the deed would be accomplished by Bettenhausen himself and his Epperly lowbelly, newly named the Autolite 5.

For some reason, Lujie cars seemed to do their best work upstairs instead of down on the bottom lane. The sensuous pink Racing Associates 3 set a track record and sat on pole position in 1959, and in 1960 was gaining on the 500's two dueling and winning Watson roadsters until it blew up. By 1961 it had metamorphosed into the Racing Associates 10 and was still fast enough to war with the Leader Card 41, one of only two Watsons with coil spring suspension. *Indy 500 Photos*

The Sarkes-Tarzian 21, Lujie's only Watson roadster clone, had a nose like a Ferrari Formula 1, and artfully upswept exhaust headers. But it was a handful. In Indy's 1962 500 it helped trigger but escaped a four-roadster smash on the 45th mile; later its dubious handling wore out two drivers; and a cockpit fire almost torched the posterior of a third, who happened to be A.J. Foyt. In 1963 the Sarkes-Tarzian covered barely 100 miles before retiring with a recurrence of the same handling ills. Missing the 500 in 1964, it returned for a last try in 1965, and on the final drop-dead Sunday of time trials bumped another dinosaur and made the show. A few moments later it got bumped itself. Then a month afterward there was a crash and another fire and it burned out at Langhorne. *Bob Tronolone*

On August 24, 1958, at the Wisconsin State Fair Park, Lujie's "bent-engine eight ball" strikes again. Rodger Ward, on the way to his and chief mechanic Herb Porter's second victory on the Milwaukee mile in one year, gets set to take a flier around the Zink Leader Card 5 of Rodger's nemesis Jim Rathmann. *Armin Krueger*

Opposite: Standing still for one of the few times in its dominating career, the Fuel Injection Special, the mighty Kurtis-Kraft with which Billy "Vookie" Vukovich became the symbol of the Offy roadster age, gets fast pit service. It won the 500 in 1953 and and again in 1954. It arguably should have won in 1952. There was never another dinosaur like it. And there was never another Vookie. *O'Dell & Shields Studios, Scalzo collection*

Dinosaur roadsters were swept out of Indianapolis in the middle 1960s when the Speedway went hell-bent for change, giving British innovators like John Cooper and Colin Chapman free rein. But demand for Lujie's and Eddie Kuzma's preternatural skills as fabricators of fine racing tackle actually picked up. Here in 1970 the two great tin men are together again in Gasoline Alley. *Bob Tronolone*

He might very well have been right, because even before weekend time trials Tony had the Autolite 5 cranking well above 149. But he interrupted his progress to go on a fool's errand shaking down his pal Paul Russo's erratic Stearly Motor Freight 24, a two-year-old Watson that had won the 500 in 1959. Apparently Russo and Bettenhausen paid a Gasoline Alley trip to Bear Wheel Alignment and put the Stearly 24 on the rack to set its front end castor, which on a Watson was controlled by a single bolt on the front axle. Russo and Tony had had this bolt off, and may have forgotten to retighten it. Whatever the case, while Tony was out track-testing the Stearly 12 again, the bolt unwound itself and fell off in the vicinity of turn 4.

Roughly 1 mile later, the Stearly 24 came honking for turn 1 hugging the outer wall and fence. When Tony touched the brakes the front axle swung out and rotated the right front wheel straight into the wall. And the Stearly 12 proceeded to do a fatal number on Tony, on itself, and even the fence, which got so ravaged that an emergency crew was up all night repairing it so that the Speedway could open again in the morning.

Of all the drivers who in subsequent seasons were in and out of the Autolite 5—Lloyd Ruby, A. J. Foyt, Jim Hurtubise, and Bobby Marshman, to name a few—nobody ever again got it blasting like

Tony had, or before him, like Parnelli and Pouelsen. Autolite 5 disappeared into history, another winless Epperly.

Quin's fifth and final laydown, the Hoover Motor Express of 1961, started from the front row with the 500's second fastest qualifying time. But while reassembling the Hoover Motor Express' Offenhauser the night before the race, its chief mechanic had somehow misaligned the Meyer-Drake camshafts. All the valves and pistons hit each other, and everything blew up in 5 miles.

The 1961 and 1962 races were the last 500s in which Quin agreed to personally help out on one of the Epperly teams. He let himself get dragged back into harness after Norman Demler at last paid him the money that was three years overdue, and then stormin' Norman tried partnering up Quin with Demler's newest firecracker driver, Jim "Herk" Hurtubise. Unfortunately, after having almost burst into the 150-mile-per-hour zone in 1960 with a facsimile Watson, Herk became well teed off when the Demler 99 Epperly lapped nearly 4 miles per hour slower. Come 1962, when the Demler 99 still wasn't much to his liking, Herk's reported dig at Quin was, "You old guys don't know how to build race cars—I'll fix it myself!" Whereupon the Demler 99 proceeded to nail the wall twice in the next two weeks.

By then worn out by all the twists and turns of roadster Indy, Quin bailed out of the 500 to begin a bizarre new phase of his unlikely career, this time constructing a Land Speed Record tricycle for rocket freak Craig Breedlove.

Lujie

Up on Figueroa Boulevard in inner-city L.A., the medic of lost-cause race cars, Ludwig "Lujie" Lesovsky, was working at his elegant peak. Certain Offy roadsters, it was claimed, found Lujie so irresistible that they'd throw fits and heave themselves against walls just to have him pay a visit with his suitcase full of long snips, short snips, drills, sanding blocks, and three dozen different hammers. Throughout the roadster years, Lesovsky earned more income modifying Kuzmas, Epperlys, Kurtis-Krafts, and Watsons than he ever did constructing his own five quirky roadsters, topped by the Wolcott 8 of 1957, a curiosity known as "the bent-engine eight ball." It was the first roadster ever to have its Offy angled across the frame from left to right—a design drawn up on a piece of shoebox cardboard on the floor of the Tropicana Hotel in Las Vegas—and it was quite likely the ultimate mile track dinosaur.

Lujie was unique. Alone among L.A.'s five builders, he was a bona fide draftsman, a skill he'd picked up in junior college while studying civil engineering. Not a temperamental artist like Kuzma, and not star-crossed like Epperly, Lujie was the rarest thing of all in dinosaur Indy: an authentic gentleman. Of Czechoslovakian blood, he maintained a dignified and almost old-world bearing, always speaking in perfectly formed accent-free sentences and using a formal vocabulary. He rarely swore, and his refined sensibilities were offended when someone else did, as happened right in Indy's pit lane in 1959. Called every four-letter name in the book by chief mechanics Herb Porter and Rocky Philipp after a suspension malfunction on the Racing Associates 3—another really fast Lesovksy lowbelly laydown and the only roadster ever painted sensuous pink—Lujie proceeded to stay home from the following season's 500 as a form of protest.

Short, stooped, mostly bald, wearing rimless glasses and later a small, elegant white mustache, Lesovsky greeted potential customers modestly. There was none of the old hard-sell in Lujie. "If you want to hire me, fine. All I can sell you is my time. I just love working on race cars."

A fanaticism for producing sturdy but light-as-possible roadsters led Lujie to use 1/4-inch bolts with tiny heads, far smaller than those used by Kuzma, Epperly, Kurtis-Kraft, or Watson. Another Lujie deal was to use worn-out issue when bolting together a chassis so that the purchaser had to personally disassemble his new roadster and replace the used bolts with fresh ones, which Lesovsky also supplied. This, Lujie once noted, had something to do with product liability and guarding himself from possible lawsuits (even though nobody in the innocent roadster era would have thought of turning a shyster on anybody else).

Frank

North of downtown L.A.'s city limits, on the leeward edge of the blue and hazy foothills of the earthquake-prone San Gabriels—the mountain range that holds all the smog around L.A.—was Glendale, home to the facilities of Frank Kurtis and A. J. Watson.

continued on page 24

Three roadsters, one of them the breakthrough Fuel Injection Special, were constructed by Kurtis-Kraft in 1952; 11 in 1953; 10 in 1954; 6 in 1955; 5 in 1956; 16 in 1957; and 7 between 1958 and 1962. But after pouring upwards of 60 dinosaurs into 11 Indy 500s, by 1963 the saga at last was over and Kurtis-Kraft constructed its final piece, the bulbous American Rubber 73. It missed the show. Afterward Frank Kurtis went off to brood about the fickleness of racing history and why other builders acquired hero status greater than his own. *Bob Tronolone*

Opposite: A. J. Watson. The young, prematurely gray "Head" of the Brickyard groove seemed to exist so that he could spend his days winning Indianapolis and bringing to life squadrons of monster Offy roadsters for he-man drivers to wrestle and car owners of spirit and wealth to bankroll. In 1963, no fewer than 8 rival teams, a quarter of the 500's 33 starters, purchased new Watson roadsters, and all but 15 of the rest of the field were either second-hand Watsons or Watson copies. But that, to Watson, was how you were supposed to race. The good-natured message that the Head was sending seemed to be, "Sure, I'll build and sell all you strokers roadsters just as fast as my own. And then my team and me will still blow you off!" *Lester Nehamkin, Mike Flaherty collection*

Above: Watson and his loyal troop of roadster-builders were a clique of no more than ten inseparable, beery, poker-playing buddies and diehard racers. They were off-the-wall, versatile, and talented. Any one of them could assemble a complete Watson roadster, paint one, plumb one, install an Offenhauser in one, construct a custom rail trailer for the roadster to be hauled away on, and then chauffeur the station wagon that was doing the hauling. Left to right: Hank Blum, the Head, and Jim Flaherty. *Lester Nehamkin, Mike Flaherty collection*

For "peace of mind" on the Speedway and on the highway I use only Firestone Tires. Pat Flaherty

1956 INDIANAPOLIS WINNER
128.490 M.P.H.

A.J. Watson had a hit with his very first design, the John Zink 8. Construction commenced in winter of 1955 and reached completion in time for the 500 of 1956. From pole position, the original Watson dinosaur got away slowly, staggered back to fourth place, then began making pass after pass to keep up. Finally it caught up to the lead Kurtis-Krafts and got into a roaring duel with them. Four hundred miles later, after leading from the 76th lap and dodging accident after accident, the John Zink 8 got buzzed by yet another Kurtis-Kraft that blew out a tire, crashed, and nearly took the John Zink 8 with it. The throttle snapped in two at the checkered flag. "We're only supposed to build these things to run 500 miles," Watson said. "That's what it did." *Mike Flaherty collection*

Opposite: New in 1959, the Simoniz 16 Watson won the first show it ever entered, the blazing fast 100 miles of Daytona Beach, run at the quickest roadster average ever, 170.261 miles per hour. At Indianapolis that same year it made the top unofficial lap of 147.06 miles per hour, qualified third, led the 500 for 48 miles, and after successfully fighting off its fellow Watson, the John Zink 64, couldn't contain the Leader Card 5 and finished second. One week afterward at Milwaukee, it gave its driver a corkscrewed back. Returning to the Milwaukee 200 two months later, it qualified fourth fastest but its original driver was still wounded from the prior spill and fell out of the seat early. An inexperienced but fast relief chauffeur was brought in to try and resuscitate the Simoniz 16, and he expertly moved it from the bottom of the standings to fourth place. Run hard through the following four campaigns as the Dowgard 2, the Coral Harbour 15, and the Drewry's Brewery, it made its farewell Memorial Day appearance in 1963 when it peeled a tire and rushed the wall. *Indy 500 Photos*

Continued from page 17

Kurtis-Kraft, located on Colorado Boulevard, had been in Glendale long enough to have probably manufactured more midget, sprint, sports, championship dirt, and Indy cars than all other builders combined. And proprietor Frank Kurtis wasn't some late-comer learning the craft of race car fabrication in the bomber facilities after the war. The son of a blacksmith, he'd served his apprenticeship much earlier, having been in the trade since 1932 when he fabricated a set of radiator shells for Don Lee, the Caddy dealer, radio broadcaster, and general race car nut. Frank had had his first car at Indy around 1935. By the beginning of 1946, he was tapping into the doodlebug craze with an assembly line of Offy midgets. Then in 1949, a Kurtis-Kraft dirt car won the American Automobile Association seasonal title, and in 1950 the same car won the 500.

In 1952, Kurtis-Kraft cranked out the Cummins Diesel, the Auto Shippers, and the Fuel Injection Special, three pioneering roadsters with elongated wheelbases, lowered bodywork, and dropped centers of gravity. They showed up at the Speedway looking like freaks among all the high-bodied dirt track cars and antediluvian front-wheel drives. Their fates varied. The Cummins Diesel was an oversized folly—out very early with a broken supercharger—though its 401 cubic inches of displacement had put it on pole. The Auto Shippers, an upright roadster, didn't start the 500. But oil man Howard Brighton Keck's Fuel Injection Special, before losing its steering and popping the wall with barely 20 miles to go, dominated and led better than three quarters of the 500. Its driver, Billy Vukovich, a national midget-racing champion, was a pedal man for the ages, and he and the Fuel Injection Special returned again in 1953 and 1954 to win by runaways. Thus the Fuel Injection Special became Indy's first, symbolic roadster.

Actually, it may not have been that good. Arriving at the Speedway 10 days late for its 1952 debut, it was immediately hailed a disaster by Howard Keck's longtime co-chief mechanics, Jim Travers and Frank Coon. They gave it the ridiculing nickname "the Toonerville Trolley." It had torsion bars behind the rear axle and in front of the front axle, and the anchor points were wrong. It had a vertical steering shaft holding two steering arms together, and its steering geometry was off too. And because Indianapolis was still, literally, the Brickyard, the track surface made the out-of-balance Fuel Injection Special a flexing spastic. Travers and Coon rescued it with remedial repairs. Because of all the loot their supportive patron Keck

paid them, the two mechanics were known as "the Rich Kids," but Jim and Frank were far richer in terms of racing savvy. Veterans of the weekly midget brawls at Gilmore Stadium and Culver City Speedway, they were used to tricking out Keck's stable of 110-inch Offys.

To overcome the flaws of the Fuel Injection Special, Jim and Frank fell back on old midget racing habits. Among other things, they "jacked weight" across its rear end, and by deliberately mis-aligning its 270 Meyer-Drake by one bolt and 36 degrees on the bell housing, they wedged hundreds of static pounds to the Fuel Injection Special's left. All this worked like a charm. Additionally, the Rich Kids and their colleague Stu Hilborn had a reputation for out-pressing everybody else when it came to making Offy horsepower.

Piggybacking on the successes of the Fuel Injection Special, other Kurtis-Krafts got into the act, temporarily turning the 500 into a Frank Kurtis benefit. They came in first, fourth, seventh, and tenth in 1953; first, third, fourth, fifth, sixth, and eighth in 1954; and first, second, third, fifth, eighth, and tenth in 1955. For the next eight seasons through 1963, when Frank made his model 500 L (for lemon), upwards of 60 Kurtis-Krafts raced at Indianapolis.

The end of Kurtis-Kraft was sad. A disgruntled and embittered Frank Kurtis turned into an awful grouch pigeonholing Kuzma, Epperly, Lesovsky, and especially A. J. Watson as thieves who stole all his roadster ideas and became heroes at his expense.

A. J.

In 1956, 2l of the 500's 33 starters were Kurtis-Krafts, but also in the line-up was a Watson roadster, the John Zink 8. It set a time trials speed record, started from the pole, and set another speed record winning the race. In 1957 and 1958 there were Epperly lowbelly laydown victories. But then the tide swung back to the upright Watsons, which won the 500s of 1959, 1960, 1962, 1963, and 1964. Their names were the Leader Card 5, the Ken-Paul, the Leader Card 3, the Agajanian Willard Battery, and the Sheraton-Thompson 1. The Bowes Seal Fast, a hybrid roadster with Watson bodywork, won the 500 of 1961. Those seven Watson scores are significant. They make the Watson roadster the most prolific Indy winner of all time, easily eclipsing such Johnny-come-lately, redcoat, carpetbaggers for the Queen of England as Lotus, Lola, and March.

Watsons monopolized the Indy grid. A 1958 sweep of the front row's three starting places was followed two years later in 1960 by Watsons filling five of the first half-dozen starting holes; a sixth roadster, the Dean Van Lines, on the pole, was a Watson reproduction. Suddenly everybody wanted a Watson, and Watson and Watson facsimiles began threatening to take over entire Indianapolis starting fields: 13 of 33 in 1961, 16 of 33 in 1962, 20 of 33 in 1963, 15 of 33 in 1964. Sweeps were commonplace. In the 500 of 1959, Watsons finished first and second. In 1961, the hybrid Bowes Seal Fast and the Dean Van Lines were first and second, with the Sun City, an authentic Watson, third. In 1962, Watsons again finished first and second with the Dean Van Lines third. In 1963, Watsons and Watson look-alikes were first, third, fourth, fifth, and

Previous pages: Waste not, want not, seemed to be the slogan of the John Zink Racing Team, which raced the guts out of its Watson roadsters and saved everything. After getting its rump bashed in and tailpipe bent up in 1958, the John Zink 16 returned to Indy in 1959 as the John Zink 64 and was in and out of first place until crashing. In 1960 it became the John Zink 28 and was in the midst of another mad run when its gearshift snapped. Sold at last in 1961, in '61 and in 1962 it raced as the Thompson Industries.

Only two other Watsons matched the Simoniz 16's five consecutive Indy starts, and one of them was the McNamara Motor Freight of 1958, which succeeded in setting a speed record and then combining with the John Zink 5 to produce the largest and worst multidinosaur wreck. Victim of a pit fire in 1959, and afterward known as the Jim Robbins, it, too, in the great dinosaur tradition, continued racing on and on and on until its last 500 of 1962. *Indy 500 Photo*

sixth. In 1964, they were first, third, fourth, fifth, sixth, seventh, eighth, ninth, and tenth. Only a total of 23 Watsons were built, and 14 of them led the 500 on 49 occasions.

Watsons battled one another like enemies. In the 1959 500, the Leader Card 5, Simoniz 16, and John Zink 64 exchanged the lead 11 times. In 1960, the Ken-Paul and Leader Card 1 topped that, swapping first place 8 times among themselves and 21 times with other roadsters. That's the way to race. In 1961, the Bowes Seal Fast chased and caught the Dean Van Lines, and they mixed it up 9 times. And in 1962, the only race cars that ever led were Watson or Watson knockoffs, the Leader Card 3, Leader Card 7, Agajanian Willard Battery, Bell Lines Trucking, and Bowes Seal Fast. What with so much intramural dueling, Indianapolis, which in half a century had experienced only a handful of close finishes, suddenly had a glut of them: the Leader Card 5 defeated the Simoniz 16 by only 23 seconds; the Ken-Paul defeated the Leader Card 1 by 13 seconds; the Bowes Seal Fast defeated the Dean Van Lines by 8; and the winning Leader Card 3 and runner-up Leader Card 7 were 11 seconds apart with the Dean Van Lines barreling down on both of them from third.

And no matter which Watson roadster it was, no abracadabra ever went into it. From 1956 through 1963, all 23 of them were constructed in three basic phases: frame building, installation of components, and fitting of coachwork.

The bomber-issue aircraft tubing was delivered in 50-foot lengths, and A. J. Watson, obeying the traditions of the era, used a ruler and chalk to mark out the wheelbase and width dimensions right on the garage floor. Before being converted into roadster spines, the main tubes had to be heated up and bent into specific dimensions—which was so easy to do, relatively speaking, that Watson, as an act of charity to out-of-work Indy race drivers during the dead-broke fall season, used to pay some of them a few bucks to do the work for him.

Next the frame skeleton was put on top of sawhorses. Then somebody, usually Watson, came around with a torch to tack on all the roadster rib cages, uprights, and cross tubes as well as the little tabs for body panels and tank brackets. Ronnie Ward, brother of the double Indy champion Rodger, usually did the welding, and when finished he cut to size the Offenhauser exhaust headers.

Then came the arrival of all the components, the whole righteous vernacular of the Watson roadster: the Halibrand racks for the

worm-and-sector steering; quick-change rear ends with splined center sections; the long steering drag links; the spindles, front axles, and brake anvils; the brake and throttle pedals and the little throttle hoops, fabricated personally by Watson; the dashboards, magnesium fire walls, instrument panels and instruments; the noses, tails, hood plates, belly pans, fuel and "can of ham" oil tanks; the Watts Linkages; the ball bearing birdcages protecting the rear brakes; the Jacob's Ladders on the right rear which let the axles move up and down instead of side-to-side; and the Panhard rod, an innocuous-looking but crucial piece of tubing located an inch or two off the bottom of the belly pan and connecting the lower left side to the lower frame rail on the right side.

"The Watson roadster is the Ford Model T of race cars!" Lujie Lesovsky once exclaimed in praise. "No trick stuff! No monkey-motion! Everything so simple, it's hard for anything to go wrong."

And Lujie was not far wrong. Exactly like old Henry and his Lizzies of tin, A. J. Watson offered for sale one basic roadster, priced between $12,000 and $13,000, take it or leave it. There were no special orders, no hocus-pocus. The Meyer-Drake Offenhauser, mounted upright, was always to the left with the driver seated on the right. The drag link connecting the steering gear bevel to the steering knuckle was also always on the right. Coachwork evolved from hand-pounded aluminum and magnesium to fiberglass, but the classic Watson silhouette resisted change. The shapely tail of the Coral Harbour 16 of 1963 looked identical to the tail of the John Zink 8 of 1956, seven years and 22 Watsons earlier. Trademarks such as the Watson cowl, the 6-foot-long Watson hood, the three-piece Watson engine mount, the 9 feet of Watson exhaust pipe, and even the dimensions of the Watson plexiglass windscreen stayed the same right down to the pattern and number of holes drilled.

A. J., during an unprecedented sprint in 1963, managed to kick out seven roadsters in barely two months. And yet he never ran his business like a platoon. All day long everybody at Watson's was laboring away on top of everybody else, torches flaring, machines sounding off, everybody jawing and joking back and forth, and then suddenly it was late afternoon and somebody was off to fetch beers. There was little formal organization, and yet the atmosphere was never out of control. On the other hand, everybody was so loosey-goosey it seems astounding, in retrospect, that anything ever managed to get built at all.

The Watson "factory," such as it existed, was at 421 West Palmer in Glendale, inside a small and fastidiously clean, white cinder-block building. Emblazoned on the front was "A. J. Watson," which was the same name that appeared on Watson's Army Air Corps papers. But the insider's moniker that Watson came to be known by among his clique at 421 West Palmer was "Head," meaning, head man, head honcho—the cool, even-tempered, onetime trailer-dolly welder who was barely in his 30s when he became the master of roadster Indianapolis.

Born in Ohio, in the village of Mansfield, Watson was the son of a devout woman who gave her children biblical names ("Abram

The Leader Card 4 Watson qualified on Indy's 1963 front row and came in fifth. The tall man timing this practice pit stop is Leroy "Birdman" Payne, one of the earliest members of the Watson clique. In addition to all the aerospace knowledge he brought to bear, most Memorial Days Leroy was the human computer/statistician standing at A. J. Watson's elbow for 500 miles. Sometimes he timed with three different stop watches at once. And he simultaneously calculated fuel economy and cooked up strategy keeping a beady eye on the most dangerous enemy dinosaurs. *Indy 500 Photos*

Joseph") and strongly suggested that they respect all people equally and not be "crabbers." She followed her own advice and lived to be an alert and calm 96. A. J.'s father was footloose, handy with his hands, and gifted at inventing things so practical that they seldom occurred to anybody else.

The old man had come to Los Angeles after World War II intending to cash in on the aerospace boom. He changed his mind, deciding that tin cans on wheels were the coming thing. Opening the Watson Dolly Company, he joined the house trailer fad.

A. J. came West to join his father. Watson had spent World War II preparing to go on bombing raids as the 20-year-old navigator of a B-17, but the fighting had stopped before he had to ship out. In Glendale, A. J.'s father acquainted him with heliarc welding. Shop classes at the local junior college schooled him in machining, and aerospace work introduced A. J. to the touret lathe.

Then one afternoon in the summer of 1946 or 1947 the Watson Dolly Company was invaded. Outside in the yard, searching for rails to tow their rods out to the Gardena Bowl or the dry lakes, weren't the usual pensioners hunting house trailer bargains but a mad gang of city hot-rodders, including such reckless and low-income teenagers as Pat Flaherty and the Rathmann brothers, Jim and Dick, who in the coming decade would send up fireworks at roadster Indianapolis. The simplicity and ingenuity of their red-blooded econo racers—the fastest L.A. rods were little but flatheads and overheads tricked out over the bare bones of bucket body Model As and Ts—blew A. J.'s mind. And as he entered the rodders' realm, the racing bug bit too. After a long and interesting apprenticeship, A. J. was still feeling the influence of those early hot rods when, in the winter of 1955–1956, he gathered his clique to build the John Zink 8.

Through the years, various worthy guys passed in and out of the Watson clique; I don't know all their names. One was Swede Johnson, a big and gruff character who used to stand in the doorway at 421 West Palmer barring visitors from entry unless they showed their "pit passes." And there was a worried-looking bugger everybody called "Miserable George," a factotum and screw-up merchant full of unfocused anxiety who nonetheless managed to make his small contribution to the Watson cause, which was all that was ever expected. There was even a Nesei pack. The Offenhauser witch and chief mechanic Chickie Hirashima, the fabricator Don Koda, and the stylist and bird dog Larry Shinoda had all been fast friends of the Okamura clan of five or six landscaping gardeners and riproaring hot-rod pilots who had lived at 421 West Palmer before the property was demolished and evolved into roadster racing's most famous address.

Of all the Watson clique, only the Head himself could be considered irreplaceable, though Wayne "Fat Boy" Ewing came close. Ewing was off-the-wall, and is worth going into at some length because the Offy roadster age wasn't only a celebration of machines but of people.

Wayne's high standing among L.A.'s racing tin men was beyond dispute, and perhaps only Eddie Kuzma could match Ewing's wonderful eye for coachwork, his knack for making race cars look fast and beautiful. In fact, his work was understood to be art. "The Fat Boy is an artist, no two ways about it," was a typical comment. "Those two hands are so talented. . . ."

Nobody quite understood how he did it, but Fat Boy, with what seemed minimal effort, could take a simple, flat sheet of aluminum and transform it into a finished Watson fuel tank or "can of ham" oil tank, or whatever. And because the Head could heliarc but not do the trickier gas welding, the Fat Boy was further irreplaceable. Just from the deftness of his movements, you could see that he'd performed the same feat many times. Torch in one hand, rod of weld in the other, Fat Boy's enormous body was elastic and quivering with interest.

He made many amazing things. He loved to sweat the details, and his coachwork for the Simoniz 16 Watson was a beautiful case in point: a complicated but stunning jigsaw puzzle of 13 separate, perfect, body panels—including the roadster's cowl, tail, front and rear belly pans, hood and side panels—held in place with 77 Dzus fasteners.

Fat Boy was obsessed with roadsters, and especially roadster noses. Supposedly it was because of him that the Watsons of 1959–1963 had no grilles but shark noses. Ewing held the opinion that previous Watson noses looked too much like those of the Kurtis-Krafts.

Fat Boy never had a driver's license, carried no insurance, never voted, perhaps never paid an income tax. The ultimate racing dropout, about the only things he ever owned other than his body tools were his radio-controlled model airplanes. Those he had a real bug for. He liked flying them in the company of his dozen children, six boys and six girls, all reputedly procreated with the same woman. As for his model airplane obsession, nobody knew how Ewing had come by it, except that, well, following the tradition of Eddie Kuzma and another one-off named Bob Pankratz, most L.A. bodymen were forgiven for being hairpins.

Fat Boy did things his own way. His downfall was that he managed to take his sweet time getting a job done. As great as his eye for detail was, he'd rarely see a project through without taking a significant detour in the middle of it. He might start making something one morning, announce he was going home for lunch, then not turn up again for a year. And he was regularly in fearful need of cash. Whenever he could, he used his reputation for peerless tin bending to extract an advance from his employer of the moment. When that didn't work, he was expert at sobbing salty tears—real tears!—about how his dozen children were home starving. Once he got any money, though, he invariably knocked off work, and the next thing you knew the cad would have his radio airplanes up in the air again. Let the kids starve!

Prior to arriving at 421 West Palmer, Fat Boy had almost run out of jobs from which to get fired. But A. J. Watson always managed to get him to report on time and do gorgeous work. Actually, more than merely gorgeous work—Ewing's Watson components were always battleship strong. All those oversized aluminum Ewing fuel

Copycat Watsons proliferated. They weren't rip-offs. The Head was so open and sharing that he never objected to loaning out roadster specs and dimensions so that Eddie Kuzma, Lujie Lesovsky, Floyd Trevis, Edgar Elder, Fat Boy Ewing, Willie Utzman, and others in the Indianapolis trade could produce substitute Watsons. Among many, there were the Dean Van Lines, the Dart-Kart, the Sarkes-Tarzian, the Vita Fresh Orange Juice, the Stearly Motor Freight 28, the Travelon Trailer, the Joe Hunt, and the Bowes Seal Fast. They kept all the merits of the bona fide Watsons, including handling, speed, and looks. Sometimes they managed to overcome the bona fides. The Bowes Seal Fast, which in truth was a medley of Watson body panels and nose, a Trevis chassis, and a whole lot of George Bignotti, won four title races including the 1961 Indy. *Bob Tronolone*

Comforting to a driver of a Watson roadster like the Leader Card 7 of 1963 was that no matter how violently the driver managed to pound a wall and collapse or squash his Wayne Ewing fuel tank, the tank wasn't likely to split open, empty out its cargo of volatile methanol, and turn into a torch job. Fat Boy built stuff strong. *Indy 500 Photos*

tanks came in as sturdy as turnplate steel. They rarely popped seams or punctured in an impact accident.

All the same, A. J. had to be careful because he had to keep Fat Boy off the model airplanes, and the only way to do that was to pay him. But then there was the risk that he might not show up for work at all. This led to the Head taking the unheard of step of paying bonuses to him whenever he completed a project on time. And the Head never teased him, as others did, about the model airplanes or tormented him by calling him "Fat Boy." Such generosity and kindness were completely new to Ewing, who was more accustomed to brutal punishment, such as having a wrathful Manuel Ayulo take him out of circulation by locking him up in a garage until he got his job done. In any event, working at 421 West Palmer seemed to stabilize and be good for him. A. J. developed so much trust in him that he could leave Ewing wandering around loose and safely go to Indianapolis not only for May but the entire summer.

Why Fat Boy finally lost his job security at 421 West Palmer was poignant, but had nothing to do with the model airplanes. Instead, it was due to the ever-increasing popularity of fiberglass in the early sixties. A diehard metal bender, Fat Boy refused to work with glass. A. J. continued using him to make fuel and oil tanks, but the heyday of the aluminum-bodied roadster had passed.

Once the Watson roadsters began sporting fiberglass noses, hoods, tails, and flank panels, A. J. enlisted the highly specialized talents of Mel le Blanc—"Mel the Fireman"—an unreformed hotrodder off the lakes who was also an L.A. firefighter. A fiberglassing wizard, and a full-on free-spirit who knew a lot about motorcycle racing, he had a reputation for flakery as storied as Fat Boy's.

Watson's clique was strong on specialized skills, but one thing that nobody at 421 West Palmer could do except Leroy Payne and Hank Blum—"the Birdmen"—was bring real engineering skills to bear. All Watson roadsters were marvels of tubing, bracing, and cross-tubing, and the two Birdmen, who were employed at Lockheed's sprawling defense complex just up the freeway in Burbank, were able to inspect a Watson's tubing network for stress tolerance in the same way that Lockheed might give the once-over to an advanced fighter aircraft. That was Leroy's and Hank's unique contribution. None of the rest of 421 West Palmer's uneducated yo-yos could read blueprints, let alone mark them up. So the Birdmen brought in some science, a trace of exotic technology.

Leroy and Hank were quite different in one way. When it came to Watson, Leroy's admiration was so over-the-top that he was on record as naming A. J. the one great mind of the whole dinosaur generation; for Leroy, a Watson roadster was race car perfection. Hank would never say that.

It wasn't anything against Watson. To the contrary, Hank was a closer friend to A. J. than almost anybody else, their friendship dating to Watson's stint as his father's apprentice at the Watson Dolly Factory.

On the other hand, Hank, with his mathematics and calculus level clear up to the sky, not only was brainy but was utterly his own man. Balding and watchful with deep-set gloomy eyes, always with smoke curling from a shortie Camel hanging out of his mouth, Hank was disdainful of big reputations, big ideas, big institutions, and all big shots in general; and he took it upon himself to speak up and try and stop the Head and everybody in the Watson clique from becoming too full of themselves. "Be humble!" seemed to be Hank's mantra.

Ironically enough, because of an unusual collaboration between A. J. and himself, Hank became indirectly responsible for making 421 West Palmer's reputation appear even greater than it already was.

It happened in 1960. In partial payment for his new Watson, the Agajanian Willard Battery, J. C. Agajanian, one of the cleverest horse traders going, had thrown in on trade one of his used Kuzmas. Unfortunately, it was one of Eddie Ka-Zoom's worst vintages, a series of Kuzma roadster that everyone was calling utterly worthless because none of them had succeeded in qualifying for the 1959 500.

All that spring the wretched automobile, minus an engine, sat around, with nobody knowing what to do with it. And then, as Hank recalls it, one day the Head asked him, "Why don't we stick the Offy out of your dirt car into it and you and I go back to the 500 as car owners?" Agreed.

Subsequently painted silver, black, and orange, and known as the Ridgewood Builders, the no-account Kuzma proceeded to make the 500, then overcome 18 other dinosaurs ahead of it and come in 13th. Counting their prize money, Hank and the Head afterward were able to sell it at a profit. Far more important, 421 West Palmer, once and for all, earned its place at the center of the roadster solar system. For if the Head and his clique had been able to make a success out of a dreadful 1958 Kuzma, they truly *were* wizards.

And poor Hank Blum, to whom all inflated reputations were an abomination, wanted to bellow in rebuttal, "But listen, Watson and I didn't DO anything to that Kuzma! All A. J. did was take out one diagonal frame bar to make it lighter! We didn't DO anything to it! It was just as good a race car as a Watson!"

No matter. In everybody's mind, 421 West Palmer seemed like a place of magic. And was.

Chapter 2
FOR THE HELL OF IT

To go Offy roadster racing at Indianapolis you had to have the scratch, the long green, and car owners who did played the most vital roles of all, because without their patronage there would have been no roadsters. Which begs the question of what in the first place made some of them fork over their money for a roadster. And the perfect answer, I suppose, was the one given by Jesse E. Rose, who has always preferred being addressed as "Ebb." Speaking for himself and I think all dinosaur owners, Ebb at first kind of shrugged. "Aw," he finally told me, "we just raced for the HELL of it." They raced for fun.

Ebb was out of Houston, Texas. Sovereign of his father's J. H. Rose Truck Lines, he was a full-blown Texan right down to his Alamo blue jeans, wrinkle-tight boots, twangy accent, and the mournful country and western music blaring out of the portable radio he listened to while sitting out on the pit wall at the Speedway. He made his first Watson roadster buy in 1963; and, to save himself the 40 percent of the purse he'd otherwise be obliged to pay one of Indy's he-man race drivers, Ebb's novel plan was to put on a set of coveralls, strap into his new Racing Associates 46, and chauffeur it himself.

Race-driving wasn't new to Ebb—he already possessed a big flashy stable of foreign sports-racing cars—but how he'd come to own his very first Indy roadster in 1960 was something of an accident. He happened to own a patch of east Texas real estate coveted by the John Zink Company. The Zinks got Rose to give it up in exchange for one of their old sleds, chief mechanic Denny Moore's version of a lowbelly laydown.

Although he passed the rookie driver test, Ebb hadn't been able to get hooked up with the Speedway and couldn't lap fast enough to qualify. Driving a second lowbelly he'd acquired, a Lesovsky copy, he

May 30, 1963. If you were the owner of an Indianapolis racing team in the dinosaur years, it never got any bigger or better or more delicious than this: you and your winning driver getting hauled around on a victory lap in the pace car your team has just won. J. C. Agajanian and Parnelli Jones live it up. *Bob Tronolone*

Rent-a-ride car owner Ebb Rose, lord and master of Rose Truck Lines, put his reputation,and his neck,on the line and put together a 148.545-mile-per-hour qualifying time trial that was so stout it blew off a third of the 1963 starting field. *Bob Tronolone*

succeeded in 1961; and then in 1962 Ebb in the same laydown again successfully qualified and came in 14th. Armed with his new Watson, Ebb in 1963 was ambitious enough to imagine piercing Indy's top ten.

Instead, he seemed in for a bad time of it. In fact, as the month of May rolled sternly along, Ebb's purchase of the Watson was looking like a serious mistake. Rose was unhappy with his Racing Associates 46. He couldn't get it lined up the way he liked, especially in the speed corners one and three. Another problem was that 1963 marked the debut of Firestone's wide rubber. Trying to accommodate himself to his Watson and its squat new Firestones was frustrating Ebb. Not even his own powerhouse chief mechanic Herb Porter could quite coach him through it. Matters became precarious.

By 4:45 P.M. of the final qualifying Sunday, the Racing Associates 46 was barely in the show at 147.2 miles per hour, slowest of all qualifiers. Weather conditions were fine. There was an hour and 15 minutes of time trials still to come. Ebb was a prime candidate to be bumped. Wonderful.

Wonderful for Rose because that nerve-wracking last hour and 15 minutes produced an unequaled opportunity for him to get ejected from the 500 and then fight his way back in all over again.

The agonies and wonders began promptly at 4:45. After taking a couple of tantalizing warm-up passes, a Kuzma lowbelly laydown bombed around for 10 miles at 148.293. That put Ebb's Racing Associates 46 on its trailer. Speedway rules are very clear about any automobile bumped from the 500 becoming ineligible to try to requalify. So not only was Ebb's Watson investment of 12 grand down the tubes, but the Racing Associates 46 would forever share an unwanted distinction with the disgraced John Zink 25 of 1957 and the John Zink 72 of 1962: the only Watsons bumped out of Indy.

The frenzy continued, and two other roadsters got bumped, one of them by a rear-engine funny car. Suddenly sharing the bubble with the identical qualifying speed of 147.620—something else that had never happened before—were two roadsters, the first an antique 1957 Kurtis-Kraft gussied up with a Watson front end and the second an Edgar Elder Watson clone.

Time was running out when time trials were enhanced by the appearance of yet another Watson, the Sheraton-Thompson 32. Ebb

Rose himself was its driver! The car owners Shirley Murphy and William Ansted were contesting the 500 with their own proven Watson hybrid, the Sheraton-Thompson 2, champion of the 500 in 1961. But all month their backup Sheraton-Thompson 32 had been at rest inside Gasoline Alley with a for-sale sign on it. Ebb wasn't purchasing it, merely renting it for the gratification of one all-out, last-gulp, qualification ride.

Ebb had several things working to his advantage. Sheraton-Thompson's assigned driver and Ebb's coach was a Houston neighbor of Ebb's—one A. J. Foyt. Equally impressive, Foyt's own chief

Tomfoolery-loving Lee Elkins, center, always made the good times roll for his mechanics and race drivers. In 1958, Dick Rathmann ("Rathman") repaid Lee for buying him this spanking new Watson by holding the hammer down and sitting big Lee's McNamara team colors on pole position at record speed. *Indy 500 Photos*

mechanic, the stalwart George Bignotti, was assisting the cause with the loan of one of his killer-diller Offenhausers. So, with backing like that—and even though it was a strange dinosaur to him—Ebb got the Sheraton-Thompson 32 going fast enough to easily put himself into the 500. Actually, that doesn't say nearly enough about Ebb's accomplishment. His smoking average speed of 148.545 was superior to a third of the starting field's.

For Ebb to have managed to do all that, and then to get to be in an official qualification photograph with A. J. Foyt, with big grins on both their faces, both hanging all over the Sheraton-Thompson 32—how much sweeter could it get for a dinosaur owner? Ebb's 500 was an anticlimax. At 37, he was one of 1963's senior participants, and he'd never made any sweeping claims of being a great race driver anyway. So he backed down his racing speed from his qualification speed by 15 miles per hour; kept his adrenaline under control for three and a half hours; missed his goal of landing in the top ten by four positions, but nonetheless traveled all 200 laps without getting into a single hot dog's way.

Lee

Attempting to sum up the motives of some of the more crazy roadster owners (I have a weakness for crazies), one of the most plugged-in personalities of the period—a funny and windy old-timer who spent plenty of Indianapolis nights at the White Front carousing with all the mechanics and drivers, and who himself was employed by various racing teams and racing companies, and who pretty much devoted his whole existence to living the Offy roadster life—once explained to me, "See, lots of those car owners were rich guys who needed a hobby. So instead of just sitting around drinking, they went racing."

Party animal Lee Elkins, lord and monarch of the McNamara Motor Freight team out of Kalamazoo, Michigan, was enlightened enough to parlay both activities, meaning he drank like a fish and went racing with a wild passion. Just for good measure, airplanes and loose females also got tossed into the mix. One afternoon in Kalamazoo, Elkins and a buddy invited some agreeable members of the opposite sex aboard a McNamara Motor Freight aircraft for the purpose of inducting them into an unofficial institution that sporting aviators refer to as the mile-high club. But after they buzzed Kalamazoo's downtown and femme undergarments rained from the plane, the city mayor, a personal friend, was forced to intervene to get good-time Lee off the hook.

Six-foot-and-190-pound Elkins was a maverick, wholly and stupendously self-made. His McNamara outfit did extremely lucrative long-haul trade with Michigan and a dozen other Great Lakes and Midwestern states, and its resources amounted to 750 pieces of rolling stock, mostly 18-wheelers, as well as 7 or 8 busy cargo aircraft.

Big Lee was a life-loving car owner who tolerated the company of only full-on race drivers—Mike Nazaruk, the ex-marine, and cruncher Dick Rathmann, to name two—and was inclined to buy

or barter race cars strictly for his employees' personal pleasure. Say that Elkins was at a racetrack where a driver who was his friend lacked a ride; it was nothing for benevolent Lee to handsomely pay off another driver to go sit up in the grandstands and drink beer and surrender his own ride to Elkins' driver friend.

With expenditures like that, along with his lust for high-stakes gambling and all the other random high costs that were vital to living what he considered the good life, happy-go-lucky Lee tended to crash-and-burn frequently. Without complaint, he'd run everything into bankruptcy, succeed in making it all the way back again, then go bust all over.

Unlike his Texas trucking counterpart Ebb Rose, Lee Elkins never developed the hots to personally race any of his various roadsters. And, for whatever reason, he seldom had a good team racing in the Indy 500; other crews objected to being downwind of the McNamara outfit because its slap-happy refuelers regularly turned their roadsters into torch jobs, including setting ablaze their Kurtis-Kraft in 1954, and then in 1956 getting it back in the race in time to hit the wall after the checkered flag.

The one season, 1958, when Lee did have a good team was something of a fluke. I will go into greater detail about it in a later chapter, but essentially, as of May 1, Lee still had no chief mechanic, no assigned driver, not even a race car. Then A. J. Watson arrived with an engineless and unpainted roadster, soon to be notorious, that he'd just completed assembling in haste. This became the McNamara Motor Freight. Following only 17 laps of practice, it proceeded to blow off all three of Watson's own John Zink roadsters and set a track record winning pole position. And on the opening lap of the 500 the McNamara Motor Freight helped bring on the biggest and most fearsome roadster wreck of all. Not only did it put itself out of commission, but also parked the John Zink 5, disabled the John Zink 16, and began the downfall of A. J. Watson's relationship with father and son John and Jack Zink. A pretty fair day's work for one roadster.

As was his way, Lee afterward shook off the memory of it all, but took what he considered prudent steps to prevent a reoccurrence. The symbols he considered lucky were 7 and 3, his dice numbers, so he slapped them onto the flanks of the rebuilt McNamara Motor Freight and in 1959 brought it back to the Brickyard again in partnership with another fun lad, Dr. Raymond Sobourin, an Offenhauser-loving chiropractor. Matters still weren't copacetic. There was the usual blown pit stop, and the crew of mechanics on the McNamara Motor Freight set on fire their Watson, its driver, and themselves. Lee Elkins then disappeared from the ranks of race car owners for the following two decades, robbing dinosaur Indianapolis of zest and unpredictability.

Bruce

One more crazy: Bruce Homeyer—just like Elkins, a dinosaur owner as well as a connoisseur of on-the-edge living, and even over-the-edge living—suffered the misfortune of having a small private airplane make him very dead in 1965. Whiskey Bruce, from what sketchy accounts were available afterward, had spent the morning getting very drunk with some drinking friends, then had gone to Caldwell Wright Airfield in New Jersey to fly his Konstant Hot twin-engine Cessna to Texas to down more spirits with still another drinking friend, the citrus king of Houston, Gordon Van Liew, owner of the Vita Fresh Orange Juice dinosaur. When a security guard at Caldwell Wright tried stopping him, Homeyer ran the guard off by threatening to whale on him with a crowbar. But although he successfully got the Konstant Hot plane up in the air, Homeyer never reached Houston; following a month's search, the plane's wreckage was discovered strewn over a wooded hill-side in rural New York. Bruce had been flying in the wrong direction.

Technically speaking, he couldn't be blamed—how could he be expected to know north from south when he didn't have a pilot's license anyway? For that matter, Homeyer also lacked a dri-ver's license. Ever since his automobile driving privileges had been revoked because he'd been apprehended tooling through New York City at 100 miles per hour, Bruce had been obliged to hire a per-sonal chauffeur. And for driving the way Homeyer instructed him to, that chauffeur had promptly lost his own license and a second chauf-feur had to be brought in to haul Homeyer around.

Bruce Homeyer owned some very fast race cars—sprinters and midgets, not just roadsters—all purchased and paid for with income from Konstant Hot, a Homeyer family enterprise occupied with the manufacture of miniature hot water heaters for coffee-vending equipment, as well as drink-ing fountains for Pepsi-Cola machines. Besides being a big dinosaur supporter, Bruce was also a wine, women, and song guy, much like Lee Elkins, but what was unfortunate was that too much sauce made him excruciatingly belligerent. He lived in exclusive Cedargrove, New

Jersey, where he had Vince Lombardi, the football coach, for a neighbor, and where, before she divorced him, he was married to a former Miss New Jersey.

Excitement and disaster seemed to travel in tandem whenever Homeyer and the Konstant Hot roadster stable showed up at Indy. There was the May, for example, when Bruce broke down a gate with a station wagon and was taking high-speed nighttime laps around the Brickyard until the entire force of Speedway rent-a-cops made him stop. And in the 1963 500, running third with 5 miles left, the Konstant Hot roadster, a Watson, made a bold and risky move, and Homeyer had to watch in dismay as his entry went spinning out of control and fell from 3rd to 15th. No Konstant Hot roadster ever performed so strongly again, and just two years afterward Bruce went on his last airplane ride.

Aggie

The rival Watson that the Konstant Hot had been maneuvering so desper-ately to overtake was none other than the Agajanian Willard Battery. It was always the roadster with the "most": most speed, most fame and infamy, and the most hexed. Year in and year out, and even during its one and only huge victory in the 1963 500, something always happened to it that made everyone else unhappy or irate. It was the roadster that ran the first official lap of 150 miles per hour and one of four that competed in the most consecutive 500s, five, all of them for the same car owner, J. C. Agajanian of Los Angeles.

Many roadsters tended to look like circus wagons whose garish liveries made statements about their various owners. Silver, cream, and red meant Lee Elkins. Ebb Rose's Racing Assoc-iates' rigs were rose (naturally) and black. Gleaming black set off by red and gold-orange sunburst trim was Bruce Homeyer and Konstant Hot. Canary yellow and black was Bell Truck Lines. John Zink was alternately pink and white or

J. C. Agajanian, the peacock of dinosaur car owners with his sharkskin suits, florid neckties, and ten-gallon lids, knew everybody and got away with everything. Every May he and his gaudy and tormenting Agajanian Willard Battery Watson, which was the first roadster to crack the sub-minute lap and exceed 150 miles per hour, seemed in the middle of giant messes and controversy. Bob Tronolone

Opposite, top and bottom: The post-race controversy of 1962 concerned all the lives that had seemingly been put at risk when the Agajanian Willard Battery, leading the 500 as ever, threw its annual fit and this time lost all its binders. And when the Indianapolis high command permitted it to continue racing anyway, demigod driver Parnelli Jones decided to go for it: "I thought, if I just stay out here and do my thing and keep out of everybody's way, who knows what'll happen?" Brakeless, he might still have won; he was leading by almost a lap, but the Agajanian Willard Battery was forced to surrender positions making pit stops, where Parnelli had to grind along the wall and bump spare wheels to stop. He still finished seventh. *Indy 500 Photos*

maroon and white, and Lindsey Hopkins was blue over red and white. But arguably the loudest eye-popper of the lot was the Agajanian Willard Battery with its explosion of shimmering pearl, gleaming white, and aggressive fire department red.

And still another vanity of certain owners was to decorate their roadsters with idiosyncratic trademarks. A humping tortoise oozing sweat and carrying on its back an insolent hare—the exact reverse of the Aesop's fable—was the symbol of Leader Card. A cowboy hat atop two fiercely pumping oil wells was the identification of the two Texas oilie cut-ups, Ken Rich and Paul Lacey. Lindsey Hopkins, himself once an amateur magician, used a whiskered white rabbit named Thurston popping from a black derby hat. But J. C.—"Aggie"—Agajanian topped them all. Always riding on the flanks of his roadsters was a caricature of an enormous and self-satisfied porker wearing a 10-gallon Stetson and the longtime Agajanian racing numeral 98. And this smug creature was depicted reclining on the back of a big rubbish truck.

It all related to the Agajanian family business out in L.A., the one that Aggie, in conjunction with his racing promotions, ran with his father and brothers. The Agajanians were a dynasty of rubbish barons and hog tycoons. And they also managed to work in a really profitable and shrewd ecological twist. On a weekly basis the Agajanian family trucks collected the used food of L.A. and afterward trucked it out to the high Mojave and the huge Agajanian desert hog ranch. There it was dined on by swine just like the one gracing the Agajanian Willard Battery.

Among car owners, J. C. Agajanian dominated the Gasoline Alley landscape of roadster Indianapolis. He was a major player; he carried considerable drag; and he was the only owner to employ a personal PR agent. A large and splashy Armenian-American with a thick mustache always trimmed just so—and who was always satirically perfect in gold sharkskin suits, florid neckties, and 10-gallon hat—Aggie was almost as impossible to miss noticing as the Agajanian Willard Battery. And equally famous and gossiped about.

Much as they all conceded that he was a great guy in most respects, certain other roadster actors like Bob Wilke of Leader Card crabbed that Agajanian was a wily fellow who too often tried using his clout and influence to his own advantage. And usually got away with it. Aggie, for instance, was known to have been the leader of the gang that railroaded out of Indy the 500's stern chief steward, Harry McQuinn, then had McQuinn replaced with Aggie's own friend Harlan Fengler. Additionally, Aggie was fast friends with all the honchos of Firestone, spending lots of time playing gin rummy with them inside the "Flintstone" warehouse at the west end of Gasoline Alley. Whispered but never proven was the allegation that because Aggie permitted Firestone's director of racing to win at cards, the Agajanian Willard Battery annually benefited from rubber goodies and speed tips that no other dinosaur got.

Agajanian, too, was on great terms with Eddie Kuzma, constructor of Aggie's 1952 Indy-winning champ dirt car. But after seasons of faithfully purchasing the hardware of Eddie Ka-zoom, Aggie and his various Kuzmas went through a miserable streak in 1957, 1958, and 1959, when they missed qualifying for three straight 500s. So, after unsuccessfully changing drivers, chief mechanics, and even his racing colors, Aggie at last had no choice but to change roadster brands. In the winter of 1959, he arrived at 421 West Palmer, Glendale, to trade in his old Kuzma for a new Watson.

Watson roadsters had a good year in 1960, but not Agajanian's—although it did put Aggie back in the show at Indy with a seventh-place finish and a Rookie of the Year accolade for Aggie's newest driver, Lloyd Ruby. For 1961, Ruby was gone and Aggie added to his stable Parnelli Jones and Johnnie Pouelsen. A lot of people who didn't much care for Agajanian, and were fed up with his seeming to get away with things, were well pleased at the 1961 Indy when at first it looked like the unlikely trio of the garbage man, the jalopy derby rookie hardcase, and the unpredictable chief mechanic was going to flop resoundingly: Parnelli at first got tripped up by the roadster neurosis of BRAKING-ITIS (i.e., braking too much).

Johnny Boyd and some of the other roadster veterans worked him through it, but early in the 500 Parnelli got hit dead-bang in the face by a flying Dzus fastener lost by one of the other roadsters. A cut opened up that covered his face with blood, then gore overflowed into his goggles.

Winds gusting through the open cockpit quickly sealed the wound, but the Agajanian Willard Battery next pitched a bitch of its own. It began running roughly. Three different pit stops to replace Offenhauser spark plugs pitchforked Parnelli 20 miles behind and at the finish the Agajanian Willard Battery got flagged off the Speedway running a well-beaten 12th. When Parnelli got to share a portion of the Rookie of the Year title anyway, Agajanian's usual detractors winked and remarked that that cunning old Aggie had used his drag to get something again.

The following year, 1962, had the Aggie detractors even more livid, this time because of a shady episode during time trials. Following their thunderous warm-up lap of 150.729, it was everybody's foregone conclusion that Parnelli and the Agajanian Willard Battery would next go on to at last crack the Indy barrier and travel all 10 qualification miles in excess of 150 miles per hour. It didn't quite happen. The Agajanian Willard Battery's opening lap was 150.150, followed by two more good laps and one weak one, and a disappointing average of only 149.492. Splitting the difference, Harlan Fengler threw out Parnelli's weak lap, granted official status to his warm-up of 150.729, and the result was the Agajanian Willard Battery's prestigious and breakthrough 150.370-mile-per-hour

---

Opposite, top and bottom: And in 1963 it was the fiasco of the oil leak, Aggie's tête-à-tête with Harlan Fengler and Colin Chapman out on the pit road, and Parnelli's one-punch encounter with Eddie Sachs the day afterward. Oozing goo, the Agajanian Willard Battery won the 500 at last. *Bob Tronolone, Indy 500 Photos*

In 1958, Jack Zink's three-Watson roadster outfit comprising the John Zink 5, John Zink 16, and John Zink 44 looked as powerhouse as Team Penske's panzer squadrons of the 1980s. All three Zinks qualified for the 500 with only two pit crews to service them. Responding to the question of what might happen if all three made a pit stop at once, builder/chief mechanic A. J. Watson deadpanned with a typical Headism: "The third guy will have to wait." *Indy 500 Photos*

record. Plus much grumbling about Indy's chief steward being under the Agajanian thumb and giving Aggie preferential treatment.

The 500 itself revved up the grumblers all over again. This time the Agajanian Willard Battery delayed raining misery down on Parnelli for 170 miles when—in the lead by almost a lap—he discovered he had no brakes. None. A freak pin prick in an aluminum brake line had allowed all the fluid to escape.

Well, Parnelli almost overcame the handicap and won the 500 anyhow. Brakeless or not, nothing managed to overtake the Agajanian Willard Battery on the racetrack, and the only time Parnelli was forced to surrender positions was while he was grinding along the pit wall, slowing down for fuel and rubber stops. Still, the best he could finish was seventh. For his part, Aggie used the occasion to initiate the practice of turning broken pieces off the Agajanian Willard Battery into jewelry: He had a sliver of the offending leaky brake line mounted on a pinkie finger ring to ruefully show people what $200,000—first-place prize money—looked like. Meanwhile, the Aggie critics moaned that Aggie had managed to get away with flaunting the rules all over again, and that no matter how brilliantly Parnelli had raced, the Agajanian Willard Battery should have been disqualified for safety reasons and hauled off the Speedway the moment Harlan Fengler had learned it was circulating without brakes.

Then came extra-controversial 1963. Just like the previous year, Parnelli started from the pole and immediately made everybody else look stupid by disappearing into a huge lead. About the only

company the Agajanian Willard Battery had to play with were three sibling Watsons, the Konstant Hot, the Bryant Heating & Cooling 9, the John Zink 52, as well as the fastest of two Ford Lotuses.

Four hundred of the 500 miles were completed when the big beef broke out. Aggie, as was his habit, was spending the 500 miles hunkered down with the rest of his Agajanian Willard Battery team behind the wall on the pit road. He was close enough to the track to feel and savor the concussion off of all the Offenhausers as they raced hell-bent up the front straightaway. And Aggie was also close enough to watch in horror as Harlan Fengler began delivering instructions to the starter of the race to get out his black disqualification flag and unfurl it in the direction of the . . . AGAJANIAN WILLARD BATTERY.

It was a short walk from Agajanian's pit stall to Fengler's chief steward station; running, Aggie made the trip in record time. Fengler's news was grim: Corner observers were radioing in to report that the Agajanian Willard Battery was spewing black goo all over the track surface! Its "can of ham" oil tank, the outboard reservoir carrying a Watson roadster's life supply of 50-weight Offenhauser lubricant, had sprung a horizontal leak.

Fengler and Aggie settled into an intense tête-à-tête while the race starter temporarily kept his black flag in its sheath. Things became heated—Aggie's 10-gallon Stetson came off so he could gesture with it. Depending on your interpretation, Fengler and Aggie were either having one hell of an argument or were merely shouting back and forth to be heard above all the Offenhausers. The version later supplied by Aggie was that Fengler was saying that the Agajanian Willard Battery was going to be thrown out for spraying oil while he, Aggie, was saying in return that the leak had long since subsided and there should be no penalty.

The two of them continued going back and forth like that, with Aggie gradually winning, when who should arrive to add his contribution to the debate but Colin Chapman, the Englishman who was the brains in back of the runner-up Lotus-powered-by-Ford. Just as Chapman was in the middle of politely inquiring when Fengler was going to have the Agajanian Willard Battery banished from the race, Agajanian cut him off: "Fengler and I are talking, Chapman. It's not your car that's in trouble." He also provided some basic Aggie-ese: "Get your ass back over the wall!"

Chapman withdrew. Fengler then gave the starter the order to forget about deploying the black flag, which the starter did. Next he took out the checkered flag, which a few laps later he was waving at the Agajanian Willard Battery.

Unfortunately, though, the 500's final miles were marked with still more extracurricular activities. The Bryant Heating & Cooling 9 had the track underneath it turn to oil and skated off onto the infield, restarted, then crashed again. And on the next to last lap, Bruce Homeyer's Konstant Hot, running a hot third and attempting to jockey ahead of the Agajanian Willard Battery and climb back on the lead lap, ran into yet another slick and itself went spinning out.

And the Agajanian Willard Battery subsequently got the blame for almost all of this   probably unfairly. Other Offenhausers in that oily 1963 500 also turned out to have been big polluters: one Watson replica, the Vita Fresh Orange Juice, finished 11th with its whole left side shiny black and with almost nothing left in the crankcase because its crew had neglected to tighten down the oil tank gaskets. Somewhat fittingly, it may have been Aggie's own garishness that did in his Agajanian Willard Battery; the red, white, and blue paint scheme made the Agajanian Willard Battery the most visible of all roadsters, and if only its oil tank had been painted black instead of pearl white, nobody might have ever noticed the leak.

The old Holiday Inn across 16th Street from the Speedway was a hostelry already famous for assault and battery among roadster personalities, and the day following the 1963 Indy was appropriately the site of a luncheon and gala to salute the 500 winners, Aggie and Parnelli Jones. After spending much of the previous 24 hours having to vigorously defend himself in the matter of Harlan Fengler and the oil leak, Aggie was fed up with it. Parnelli was feeling equally testy. Fatefully present at the same banquet—and eager to tell the world that they'd gotten the shaft from Aggie, Parnelli, and Fengler, and the Agajanian Willard Battery's oil were the Bryant Heating & Cooling 9's chatterbox driver Eddie Sachs, along with the roadster's equally assertive chief mechanic, Wally Meskowski.

Sachs and Meskowski confronted Aggie and Parnelli, or perhaps it was the other way around. It was very close to turning into a brawl. Each one of them was ready to hit at least two of the others.

Sachs at last called Parnelli a name, Parnelli threw a punch, and Sachs went down. The chief mechanic Meskowski called Agajanian a name and Aggie thought it behooved him to throw a punch of his own, but he didn't. When Sachs instead of Aggie's boy Parnelli afterward got fined and put on probation for a year, a lot of people thought Aggie had again escaped blame he richly deserved. Many wished that Aggie had gone ahead and taken a punch at Wally Meskowski because then Aggie himself might have ended up on probation or suspended from racing. Well, perhaps he might have been, but it was equally certain that Wally would have suffered pain. When he had to be, Aggie was quite a puncher.

And that was the unsurpassed, when they made-him-they-broke-the-mold J. C. Agajanian. As a younger man, he'd harbored fantasies of becoming a race driver himself. Judging from the hell-on-wheels manner he handled mundane highway chores, Aggie perhaps really thought he was one. Hurtling to one of his race promotions, he once got his Cadillac out of control and upside down and a director of the U.S. Auto Club, who was Aggie's passenger, ended up in a neck brace. Following yet another traffic altercation, this one in L.A., Aggie himself ended up with broken ribs and lacerations. One tough stud, he checked himself out of the hospital to go back to work. In any event, the memory of Aggie out there on the Indianapolis front straightaway getting in Harlan Fengler's face and standing up for his hexed Agajanian Willard Battery, and for the great Parnelli Jones, and in the process telling off Colin Chapman—all superior upper-class teabagger manners and treachery—all those

A. J. Watson's all-Watson roadster front row of 1958. So what's wrong with this picture and why is it an "Oops!"? Because the Head somehow allowed pole position to slip away from his own John Zink team and instead be won by the opponent Watson roadster of Lee Elkins. The other man in the picture is car builder and Elkins chief mechanic Floyd Trevis. *Indy 500 Photos*

things and more perversely make J. C. Agajanian my favorite owner/hero of the Offy roadster.

Jack

Aggie loved being where the action was. One time at a championship match up at Milwaukee, he came right over the pit wall with his refuelers to enthusiastically help out on a pit stop. This carried hazards, of course. In 1964, the Agajanian Willard Battery—newly named the Agajanian Bowes Seal Fast—made a spectacle of itself for the last time at Indy by blowing up and burning out with a reverberating alcohol explosion that ripped open its tail and launched a foot-square section of fuel tank that had been secured by 30 bolts just past Aggie's head.

There was another worthy individual who shared Agajanian's belief that safe and sane and out of harm's way behind the pit wall was no place for a hot-blooded owner of a roadster. If you study closely the documentary film of the 500 of 1956, the Memorial Day of the John Zink 8's breakthrough Watson win, you'll notice that during pit stops this particular car owner is doing something that an owner seldom did, which is get out there on the pit lane and physically replenish the right rear Flintstones of the John Zink 8 all by himself. There was nothing of the ne'er-do-well about Jack Zink.

Born in Tulsa, Jack graduated from Oklahoma State with a mechanical engineering degree and immediately went to work in his hometown for his father's John Zink Company, manufacturer of floor heaters, unit heaters, and industrial burners. John Zink was a jovial and grossly fat patriarch who consumed beer by the crate and cut quite a figure around the Speedway with his short pants, high-top sneakers, tentlike shirt, and annual entourage of 150 jolly fellow Okies imported from Osage County.

While his daddy was busy socializing and entertaining, Jack was supervising the operation of the John Zink team. Jack was smart. In fact Jack was the shrewdy who had had the perspicacity to hire A. J. Watson as Zink chief mechanic for the 500 of 1955, the year when three almost-boy wonders became the rage of Victory Circle: The Head was 30; Bob Sweikert, chauffeur of the winning John Zink Kurtis-Kraft was 29; and Jack Zink at 27 was youngest of all.

That same 1955 winter, Watson began construction of the John Zink 8. Considerable confusion and differing recollections among the parties involved, plus outright misinformation, still cloud the project.

One thing wrong is that people still believe that the John Zink 8 was the very first Indy roadster that A. J. Watson ever built, when actually Watson and his former colleague-partner Jud Phillips had collaborated on an underfinanced yet surprisingly successful

econo-dinosaur a season earlier. Another thing wrong is that Watson is often credited with having been clairvoyant about what 1956 conditions at Indianapolis would be like, and that the John Zink 8's design deliberately took advantage of the Brickyard's new smoother and faster surface. But during a 1995 conversation we had, Watson informed me that he really hadn't been that smart. He also stated unequivocally that, yes, the John Zink 8 and all 22 of the other Watson roadsters were heavily influenced by design features of the Kurtis-Kraft. Using the Kurtis as something to go by, Watson had first eliminated almost 75 pounds of reinforcement plate, then narrowed and lowered the chassis and redistributed the weight by pulling the motor plate back 6 inches until it was right in the middle of the wheelbase. Contrasting the obvious difference between a Kurtis-Kraft and a Watson, a dinosaur personality and sharp observer named Nat Reeder once put it this way: "You see all the extra reinforcement and heaviness of a Kurtis-Kraft compared to a Watson? Frank built his roadsters to last a whole racing season. A. J. made his to go 500 miles."

Occasionally, too, you hear reports that Jack Zink personally insisted on having a lot to say about the design of the John Zink 8. It's not unlikely. Jack was paying Watson's bills and used to frequently travel out to L.A. and spend time at the Head's first shop on Gardena Street in Glendale. Unique among other owners of roadsters, Jack was in possession of an engineering diploma. In other words, he was the only patron who had the qualifications to second-guess Watson and even maybe Watson's brainy Birdmen, Leroy Payne and Hank Blum.

As mentioned previously, instead of having Watson hire some big gorilla to change the John Zink 8's right rears during its winning 500 of 1956, Jack demanded the privilege of going out there on pit road and having the fun of performing the work himself. Also, somewhat in the manner of J. C. Agajanian, Jack occasionally put on automobile-racing promotions and even daydreamed of being a race driver. Already quite an accomplished drag strip hound, Jack was on the verge of going much, much further, and—before his father stopped him in his tracks—was preparing to construct and pilot his very own Land Speed Record projectile. During one of his dirt track promotions in Oklahoma, an extravaganza for NASCAR convertibles, Jack casually borrowed somebody's rag top and succeeded in lapping faster than Fireball Roberts and Lee Petty.

Bob

During his four-year relationship with Watson, Jack Zink ended up with inventory of four roadsters. They were the Indy-winning John Zink 6 Kurtis-Kraft of 1955, the Indy-winning John Zink 8 Watson of 1956, the John Zink 52 Watson of 1957, and the John Zink 16 Watson of 1958. Only one other owner ever possessed more individual Watsons, and he was Bob Wilke, who had seven. They were the Leader Card 5, the Leader Card 1, the Sun City, the Leader Card 41, the Leader Card 3, the Kaiser Aluminum 1, and the Leader Card 7.

"Well, we drink beer early today," was roadster owner shorthand for when everything had gone to hell and you and your team were out of a 500 early. Broken and dead at 335 miles in 1960, the John Zink 28 gets pushed toward Gasoline Alley by its mechanics and owner Jack Zink, wearing the beret. *Indy 500 Photos*

The Leader Card 5 and the Leader Card 3 both won Indianapolis 500s. The Leader Card 1 ran second in 1960, which was the hottest dinosaur 500 ever. The Sun City came in third in 1961, and the Kaiser Aluminum 1 was fourth in 1963. A year after its unsuccessful debut, the Leader Card 41, renumbered the Leader Card 7, took second in 1962. In 1963, a year after winning Indy, the Leader Card 3, now the Leader Card 4, finished the 500 fifth; two years after that in 1965, now known as the Wynn's Friction Proofing 5, it went to Phoenix International Raceway and proceeded to score the final dinosaur victory.

Over time, Wilke sold off some of his used Watsons, and most of them went on doing well. Harry Allen Chapman of Tucson, Arizona, became custodian of the Leader Card 1, and it turned into a five-time Indy 500 starter, as well as going to Hanford, California, in

1968 and achieving posterity as the last Offy roadster to qualify for a starting berth in a championship race. The worst of all Wilke's sales involved the Leader Card 5, which was purchased by Stearly Motor Freight, and in 1961 crashed and took out Tony Bettenhausen.

Bob Wilke was short and stocky, a curly-haired little bulldog of a man constructed somewhere along the lines of Rodger Ward, Leader Card's long-standing star chauffeur. Bob was active in the association of Indianapolis car owners, and decades before personally coming to the Brickyard had been one of the premier movers and shakers of midget car racing. As the Midwestern distributor of both the Offenhauser 110 and the Kurtis-Kraft midget, Bob had sold hundreds of both things, as well as spent almost $2 million campaigning them.

Leader Card, the Milwaukee, Wisconsin, paper productions corporation responsible for Bob Wilke's substantial wealth, distributed

It never had happened before and never would again. Leader Card's sweep of first and second place in the 1962 500 was the only time one dinosaur team enjoyed such a stranglehold. Winner Rodger Ward (foreground) and runner-up Len Sutton mug it up the morning after. Standing, left to right, Leader Card czar Bob Wilke, Ward chief mechanic Watson, and Sutton chief Chickie Hirashima. *Bob Tronolone*

Certain dinosaur car owners thought that they had a special knack for divining talent. Bob Wilke was one, and his driver choices could be utterly unpredictable. One night at the White Front saloon he'd get into a casual conversation with some shoe he liked, and the following morning be telling Watson that he was going to make the guy a Leader Card employee. The unpredictability caused misunderstandings. Johnny Boyd, here with Wilke in 1961, assumed that in 1962 he was going to be back at Leader Card. When he instead got fired and replaced by Len Sutton, Johnny erroneously assumed that Len had gotten the ride by scheming against him. Consequently Johnny decided to never speak to Sutton again, and didn't, for the next 30 years. *Indy 500 Photos*

everything from envelopes to announcement cards to poker decks. In contrast to the hot and for-the-hell-of-it mentality of an Ebb Rose, Bob was more in the tradition of the cold and unsmiling bottom-line businessmen Indy car owners of the nineties. He shunned the limelight, rarely gave interviews, and apparently genuinely objected to flash and glitter. Dinosaur roadsters were almost obliged to have their garish liveries, but Leader Card colors were innocent—ice box white with red-and-black numerals, although sometimes Larry Shinoda got permission from Bob to throw on some extra light.

Despite his low profile, Wilke ranks as the most opportunistic dinosaur owner of all. For Bob was the guy who stepped in and hired Watson just as the Head's four-year-long association with the John Zink team was unraveling.

Exactly how and why this unraveling occurred is one of the most talked-about tableaus of Offy roadsterdom. The version most frequently given is that toward the end of 1958, Jack Zink had issued an order that A. J. pull up stakes from Los Angeles and move the headquarters of the John Zink team to Tulsa. He may have given this order because he honestly felt he could provide A. J. with a superior racing facility there, or maybe because it was hard keeping Watson under control while he was operating out on the coast 1,500 miles away. Whatever the reason, this story continues, A. J. reacted to Zink's ultimatum that he quit his beloved Glendale and abandon his faithful roadster clique by throwing a car builder's mutiny and handing Jack his immediate notice.

While this explanation sounds plausible, it isn't what happened. Far from balking at Jack Zink's demand that he move, A. J. initially complied so thoroughly that he put his Glendale home on the market. And had he not next run into Bob Wilke, the Head would have been on his way to Tulsa.

As A. J. tells it, he and Bob had a meeting that was so unexpected and it must have been destiny that arranged it. Here's what happened: A. J. was in a telephone booth—he thinks it was one of the pay phones inside Gasoline Alley—informing Jack Zink that his home had just sold. Finished with the call, he stepped out of the booth and literally bumped into Wilke as Bob came strolling past.

A. J. and Bob already knew one another well because during the 1958 summer Wilke had co-sponsored the John Zink 5 when it was shipped to Italy and won the Race of Two Worlds at Monza. Bob, in fact, had once offered A. J. a chief mechanic's job. Now, on a wild impulse, A. J. asked him if he'd truly meant it.

The two men met again not long afterward in Chicago, where Wilke was attending a paper convention. A. J. came back from their meeting not with "a lifetime contract," as has been claimed, but with a new Pontiac station wagon tow rig, a budget of $50,000, and Wilke's mandate to win Indy for Leader Card.

Bob didn't force Watson to move to Wisconsin and resettle in Milwaukee, the Leader Card base, but encouraged him to purchase a new home out in L.A. Watson also was supposed to vacate his longtime Glendale shop on Gardena Street—a new freeway was going through the property—and move to his new works at 421 West Palmer. But then a crisis broke out, and it was the sort of thing that could only have happened to the Head. Typical of the whole casual way he operated, A. J. had never bothered to put on paper any wheelbase or other roadster dimensions, every year preferring instead to just go by his old chalk marks on the cement floor at Gardena Street. But Gardena Street had been razed for the freeway, and A. J.'s ex-employer Jack Zink had three of the four existing Watson roadsters back in Tulsa. So how was A. J. going to remember how to construct a new roadster for Leader Card?

Well, by sheepishly telephoning back East to Lee Elkins, custodian of the only other Watson roadster then in existence, the McNamara Motor Freight. The fabricator and designer Floyd Trevis was Lee Elkins' chief mechanic, and Floyd was good enough to copy down and send out to Glendale all the measurements so that A. J. could get on with building the Leader Card 5.

And then everything good happened. From 1957 through 1958, no Watson roadster had won a paved track race, including the 500, and there had been conjecture that lowbelly laydowns might be the way to go at Indy. But from 1959 through 1963, the "three Ws" of Wilke, Watson, and Rodger Ward became the premier dinosaur team. Besides their Indy victories of 1959 and 1962, the Leader Card trio also finished second, third, and fourth in the 500s of 1960, 1961, and 1963. During those same years, the three Ws additionally accumulated two seasonal national championships, three times got second, and once were third. There used to be a point standings award for the top national champion car owner, too, and Wilke won it twice.

Jack Zink had possibly wanted A. J. in Tulsa to keep a closer eye on him, and to prevent him from springing any more surprises like in his spare time constructing the McNamara Motor Freight, which had cost the Zink team the 1958 pole position and perhaps a victory in the 500. Yet Wilke never put constraints on Watson when it came to constructing roadsters for teams other than Leader Card. Even when Watson agreed to make the Willard Battery for J. C. Agajanian, a car owner Bob didn't like, as well as the Ken-Paul, the rival Watson roadster that succeeded in blowing off Bob's own Leader Card 1 and winning the 1960 500, no ruckuses were raised by Bob afterward.

In their dealings together, in fact, Bob gave A. J. almost a free hand. Throughout the Leader Card years, Watson got paid a weekly salary, plus a flat 20 percent off the top of everything, including all prize money and roadster sales. Bob had once suffered a powerful heart attack he was years recovering from; perhaps he was under medic's orders not to act up and leave behind crazy stories like the ones dinosaur folks still occasionally tell about Lee Elkins and Bruce Homeyer. And this low profile may have been the characteristic that made Wilke the dominant roadster owner. He was seldom there interfering or staring over A. J.'s shoulder; instead, Bob simply trusted the Head to run Leader Card as he saw fit. According to A. J., that day in 1958 in Chicago when they made

Bill Forbes, left, namesake of the Bill Forbes Racing Team, and his boy chief mechanic Dave Laycock, did the right thing in 1962 when they purchased their Watson, the 15th of the 23 that the Head built. It wasn't one of the lucky dozen that won at least one championship race, but in Forbes livery and later that of Weinberger Homes, the car started in 18 such matches, including finishing 4 Indy 500s. It was in the thick of the 1962 fight to exceed 150 miles per hour at the Speedway; in 1963 it lapped at a then-record 186.329 miles per hour on a tire-testing bowl in Texas; and it finished fifth and became the last front-engine to complete all 200 laps at Indy in 1965. And that same year it occupied pole position at Langhorne with a new time trials record against funny cars. *Indy 500 Photos*

Rich was a happy-go-lucky wild-catter who'd made his pile from under the earth. And when not involved in sniffing out oil and natural gas from Texas and Louisiana, or going far out into the Gulf of Mexico to hunt for it with monster drilling rigs, Kenny was headquartered in Dallas where he maintained good-buddy relations with what seemed like every fellow high-end wheeler-dealer in big D.

One of them was Paul Lacey, Kenny's partner in a wide and impressive variety of business enterprises. Lacey happened to be one of the most successful commodities brokers in the state. So excellent was Paul at this, in fact, that during the seventies, when the silver-buying scheme of Nelson Bunker Hunt and William Herbert Hunt was going down—the Hunts, you may recall, were attempting to highjack the market—it was well remembered in some high-dollar circles of Dallas that Paul had been the insider who originally steered his Texas pals, the Hunts, into precious metals.

Around Christmastime of 1959, Kenny and Paul were lunching together at a monument of oil patch Dallas called the Petroleum Club. Kenny suddenly declared that the two of them must purchase a roadster

Lindsey Hopkins, in the cockpit of his Dowgard Special with his 1960 driver Tony Bettenhausen, was a jolly investment banker-cum-Southern aristocrat who dabbled at magic and reputedly had the biggest bundle of all dinosaur owners. He was on record as saying that racing should be an elegant, exotic pastime and never a dog-eat-dog greedy business. Winning the 500 demanded prerequisites besides barrels full of bucks. Lindsey and his whiskered mascot Thurston the bunny rabbit never made it into Victory Circle. *Indy 500 Photos*

their simple arrangement and sealed it with a handshake, Bob told him, "I'll take care of the bills, you take care of the team." And added, "Only buy the best."

Kenny and Paul

Next to the fun Ebb Rose got out of actually getting to race a roadster in the Indy 500, my hunch is that Kenny Rich and Paul Lacey derived more pleasure and sheer bang-for-their-megabucks with their 1960 Watson, the Ken-Paul, than all other owners.

Rich and Lacey were a pair of high-rolling and good-time dudes of a classic Texas sort. While Rose had derived his Houston trucking money from the big rigs of his daddy's diesel squadrons, Kenny

together and use it to win the Indy 500. There may have been a bit more to it than that, of course, but essentially, Kenny was telling Paul, who'd never so much as seen an automobile race before, "C'mon, we'll pool our money and have some fun!" They'd already done plenty of fun things together, but this was going to be special.

Naturally they wanted the best, and only a Watson roadster would do. And, as Texas luck would have it, Rich and Lacey ended up buying one of the Head's 1960 series, the best roadsters ever to come out of 421 West Palmer. And the Ken-Paul became the only Watson that A. J. ever charged extra for—the ultimate price tag of the Ken-Paul was better than $15,000—because, in Texas oilie tradition, Kenny Rich had asked for various extra touches.

"A. J. asked me what color I wanted it painted," Rich recalled, "and I told him that blue was my favorite and to make it a really pretty shade. Where A. J. got the paint and all, I don't know, but we ended up with the prettiest car in the 500 that year."

The celebrated supporting cast hired at top wages to perform the Ken-Paul's driving and maintenance was an incredible one. The driver was Jim Rathmann, who'd previously taken close seconds in three 500s, and who'd gotten the go-ahead by Rich and Lacey to run the whole shootin' match. Whomever Rathmann told them to hire they did, including Chickie Hirashima, who took a hiatus from A. J. Watson to sign on as the Ken-Paul's mechanic, and to plot race day strategy, Smokey Yunick, renowned for coordinating some of the fastest pit stops in stock car racing.

Throughout the three-month gestation period of the Ken-Paul, Kenny and Paul paid many visits out to California to see how the work was progressing. Just so they wouldn't get lonely out in faraway L.A., they often brought along for companionship various male and female Texan buckaroo buddies. And because travel all by itself could be a bore, the charter plane might first touch down in Las Vegas, whose various attractions could delay the arrival in L.A. for a week or more.

The month of May commenced. Less upscale teams in the 1960 500 were outfitted in their usual down-at-the-heels Mobil or Firestone T-shirts; the Ken-Paul tribe sashayed around in smashing custom outfits turned out by ritzy Neiman-Marcus. And in a block of 30 rooms and suites commandeered for the Ken-Paul entourage, Kenny and Paul took up giddy residence at the Speedway Motel.

Other roadster owners, on the other hand, had all the luck. Shirley Murphy and William Ansted, the Sheraton and the Thompson parts, respectively, of the Sheraton-Thompson team, purchased a spare Watson roadster in 1963. For the most part these 1963 models turned into the Edsels of the Watson line—responsible for backing into walls, getting bumped from Indy starting lineups, going endo on road courses, and performing other extremely self-destructive acts. Sheraton-Thompson's lemon got rented out to Ebb Rose for Ebb's big qualifying deal of 1963. Afterward, it was quietly parked again. Yet in 1964 the machine roared back into action as the almighty Sheraton-Thompson 1. It won at Phoenix, Trenton, the Indianapolis 500, and Milwaukee: four championship meets in a row, something no other race car of any era may have accomplished. That fall at Trenton it added its fifth win and set a speed record on its fourth different speedway, becoming the greatest dinosaur winner of all time. *Bob Tronolone*

Strong Texas accents rang out. The free-spending, large-living Hunt brothers were in regular attendance, as were Stanley Marcus, Clint Murcheson, and various land barons and bankers—half of high-society Dallas must have been bivouacked out there next to turn 1. Beauty queens, dishy airline stews, and lots of friendly cowgirls revved up the atmosphere. Doing the wine, women, and song number around the clock could tax even a Texan, but occasionally Kenny and Paul would depart the suites, bar, swimming pool, and other pleasures of the Speedway Motel to frolic over to the Brickyard and observe their sweet blue Ken-Paul cutting some of the month's fastest practice laps.

The subsequent 1960 race became the wildest roadster Indy ever. One Lesovsky lowbelly laydown managed to lead for a few miles, but this 500 was the crowning moment of the Watsons. Four of them, including the Ken-Paul, went at each other; first place changed hands 30 times. The Leader Card 1 led, the Dean Van Lines led, the John Zink 28 led, the Ken-Paul led, the Leader Card 1 led, the Dean Van Lines led, the Ken-Paul led, the Dean Van Lines led, the Ken-Paul led, the Dean Van Lines led, the Ken-Paul led—and throughout the final, galvanizing, 140 miles, the Ken-Paul and the Leader Card 1 chased each other down the track.

Kenny and Paul were too overexcited, nervous, and, well, plastered, to watch the duel, instead passing the 500 miles wandering numb and disoriented through the crowds at the Tower Terrace, in and out of Gasoline Alley, over to the first corner, and then back again. When in their confusion they got separated, Paul's only means of following the 500's progress was via the public address system, whose announcers were going berserk.

So caught up in the whole frenzy of wondering and worrying and listening did Paul finally become, that in the closing laps while he was visiting one of Gasoline Alley's latrines, he forgot totally where he was and what he was doing. Hearing one of the janitors shouting, "Mr. Lacey!, Mr. Lacey!" he glanced up abruptly. Low and behold, he was lined up to take a whiz not into the urinal but a wash basin.

Meanwhile, from the message over the PA, he realized he had just missed the 500's deciding moment. The Ken-Paul had at last run the Leader Card 1 out of rubber and was pulling away.

All the pandemonium of Victory Circle was a ho-hum prelude to what followed back at the Speedway Motel where some of the hardest-drinking, larger than life, vintage Texans ever put on earth were preparing to break out the booze and barbecue and put on a roaring winners' party to show the Hoosiers how to celebrate.

Beginning with simple hand-shaking and back-slapping and a few essential "Yahoos!" the atmosphere escalated and gained force until Texans and Hoosiers alike were leaping into the swimming pool with their clothes on or else getting tossed in that way.

Kenny did. Paul did. And so did perhaps the richest man in the U.S. then, Bunkie Hunt. When the manager of the Speedway Motel arrived to try and restore order, he, too, went in; however, evicting from the premises the entire Ken-Paul group in retaliation was out of the question. There was the consideration of all its lodging, liquor, and overall entertainment bills—already the equivalent of the team's first-place prize money—and, besides, the party was just getting good.

Indianapolis roadster owners, really, never were supposed to have this kind of fun. They were expected to bring all their money and then stay away, leaving the racing and the fun to the racers. So Kenny Rich and Paul Lacey succeeded in double-crossing everybody! I love it that the mightiest roadster victory of them all should go to the pair of car owners who also happened to be the most for-the-hell-of-it guys of all.

"That buckaroo party of yours went on all night?!" I once asked Kenny.

"Party went on about two days, actually," he corrected me, sounding nostalgic.

I regret having to add that Kenny and Paul both ended up in the divorce courts, their wives turning out to be not the kind of Indy 500 fans and party animals that the husbands were. But I wish that Texas party at the Speedway Motel was still running.

Hide the women and children, here come the Texans. Jim Rathmann, chauffeur of the Ken-Paul roadster, won the amazing 1960 500, the most blistering speed duel of the dinosaur age. Meanwhile his good-time car owners Kenny Rich and Paul Lacey, two of the lone star state's wildest buckaroos, redefined the boundaries of how far roadster owners could go in search of fun. *Indy 500 Photos*

Chapter 3
WHITE FRONT NIGHTS

For every May of the roadster years, the fanatically inbred and competitive racing society of Los Angeles emptied almost all its members back to Indianapolis. By Memorial Day, the few L.A. personalities who weren't back at the Brickyard were home glued to the radio listening to yet another 500 being won by their brother builders, drivers, and, especially, chief mechanics. L.A. chiefs won 14 consecutive Indys.

Getting set for his haul across the continent, the first thing an L.A. chief had to do was roll his dinosaur onto its rail trailer, then load up the station wagon tow car with all the paraphernalia of the roadster, including the bulky aircraft-type starter for the Offenhauser and all the battery carts and toolboxes. Next the chief set out on old Route 66, the hot road back to Indy, without stopping until making the Speedway entrance on 16th Street and Georgetown. One of his first duties upon arrival was to scrub the roadster body panels and fire walls clean of accumulated highway salt.

Working on a roadster wasn't rocket science, but the duties piled up as the month progressed. A chief mechanic had to know how to set castor and camber, swap gear ratios, preload the frame's reverse-weight, disembowel a Meyer-Drake and correctly reassemble it again, plus maintain the transmission, disc brakes, spindles, torsion bars, steering arms, open-tube Halibrand quick-change, and the several dozen additional components that comprised a dinosaur.

This was the grunt work, the no-brainer stuff. The chief's tricky and really difficult responsibility was to watch, clock, critique, and make certain that

Kuzma, Epperly, Lesovsky, and Kurtis-Kraft worked soley in the construction and repair end of Indy cars. But by functioning in the dual role of builder and chief mechanic, A. J. Watson got his jollies down and dirty in the pits of Indy and the national championship tournament, in the thick of the racing. This meant that every Watson roadster he constructed had to be all buttoned up in time for the Head to depart for the Speedway that May.
Lester Nehamkin, Mike Flaherty collection

Every 500 during dinosaur Indy was won by an L.A. chief mechanic, with four different chiefs accounting for eight different wins between them. A. J. Watson collected half of them, those of 1955, 1956, 1959, and 1962. George Bignotti won in 1961 and 1964. Johnnie Pouelsen won in 1963. And Chickie Hirashima, snoozing here inside the Leader Card 7, 1962's runner-up, won in 1960. *Indy 500 Photos*

something so big and grossly heavy as his roadster could practice and barrel around and around the 13,200 feet of the Indianapolis Motor Speedway. The roadster had to knock off only 30 miles per hour or so from its 170 top end, and then make it safely around all four narrow, 1,320-foot corners without swaying, pitching, or hurling its driver into the wall.

A chief could jack around with how his roadster handled in a number of ways. He might experiment with the suspension hardware, including the shocks and sway bar, or he could redistribute the approximate dead-weight ton of weight by wedging the torsion bars. This was how chief Buster Warke preloaded his Dayton Steel Wheel, a two-year-old Watson, which Troy Ruttman successfully qualified for the 1964 500 at 151.292 miles per hour:

Left Front	Right Front
421 pounds	355 pounds

Left Rear	Right Rear
970 pounds	584 pounds

The Dayton Steel Wheel was a much-abused Watson, and more than those of a Kuzma, Epperly, Lesovsky, or Kurtis-Kraft, every component of a Watson was adjustable, easily adjustable. All chief mechanics liked that. A. J. Watson, of course, was unique among the five builders because he was the only one of them who also worked as a chief mechanic. Not only that, but in the unlikely event that one of the other chiefs couldn't solve some Watson problem, the Head, in his role of designer, was always around to help sort the difficulty. This made Watson

either a saint or a sucker: In at least two 500s he so successfully helped opponent Watson roadster teams that they managed to defeat A. J.'s own John Zink and Leader Card teams. Still, for as long as he built roadsters, Watson went on routinely sharing and pooling speed tips with the opposition, his customers. This meant that he was always racing against himself. Yet the Head still won four Indys, the record for L.A. chiefs.

*W*inning the 500 was everybody's goal. Obviously. Yet making it such a hard job was the fact that dinosaurs were so equal, especially the Watsons. All their drivers were equal too. So developing an advantage over everybody else was another responsibility of a chief mechanic. The best ones truly could make a difference.

Consider Johnnie Pouelsen. From 1961 through 1964 he did four Indys with J. C. Agajanian, Parnelli Jones, and the trio's snakebit Watson, the Agajanian Willard Battery. This difficult automobile finally won the 500 of 1963, but minus all its bitterly frustrating breakdowns could have won two others. Johnnie at one time wanted to quit. He was a strange hombre anyway, and once, to recover emotionally from another defeat, was said to have exiled himself to Chicago's O'Hare airport where he sat brooding in the lobby for three sleepless days and nights. Often you could ask Johnnie a question and, because he was either deep in thought or just indifferent, get no answer.

Moody or not, Johnnie was really on the ball. In the 1963 500, the year of the big oil controversy, when Johnnie's Agajanian Willard Battery was under attack from a mob of fellow Watsons as well as being stalked by one of the Ford-powered Lotuses, Pouelsen improvised the victory strategy of preserving Parnelli's lead by scheduling all the Agajanian Willard Battery's refueling stops to coincide with yellow slowdowns on the track.

A. J. Watson was responsible for a pair of victory-saving efforts of his own. In the win of the Leader Card 5 in 1959, Watson at 117 miles orchestrated its first refueling and rubber stop under yellow conditions; at 250 miles conducted a lightening green flag stop; and with 80 miles to go carried out the Leader Card 5's crucial last stop under yellow. As a result, the Leader Card 5's winning advantage over the worthy runner-up, the Simoniz 16, was 23 seconds.

Three years afterward in 1962, when Watson's Leader Card 3 and Chickie Hirashima's Leader Card 7 were both being made nervous late in the 500 by Clint Brawner's onrushing Dean Van Lines, Watson and Hirashima combined to concoct the strategy to rescue

Extra close chief mechanic-driver friendships like that between Parnelli and Pouelsen were rare. The average chief held his distance because the relationship could terminate abruptly. Concerned that a driver might be sticking out his neck too far, chief Buster Warke had the habit of observing him lighting a cigarette after getting out of the car; if his hands shook, Buster was concerned. Placing his palm on a driver's backside checking for undue perspiration was chief Smokey Yunick's ritual. But sometimes nothing could save a race driver from himself. George Bignotti lost Jimmy Reece at Trenton, above, in 1958, and George Amick in 1959 at Daytona; Jud Phillips lost Al Keller in 1961 at Phoenix and Don Branson at L.A. in a sprint car in 1966; and A. J. Watson in 1960 lost Jimmy Bryan at Langhorne. *Bruce Craig*

Leader Card and save the stable's one-two finish. Similarly but less successfully in 1958, Watson had attempted to rescue the John Zink 16. After getting nailed in its hindquarters on the very first lap, No. 16 had reached the pits bedraggled and requiring Watson's emergency repairs. It received them, then finished a low-flying sixth. Watson had the consolation of knowing that minus all those unscheduled minutes it had sat on pit road getting overhauled, the John Zink 16 actually spent less time on the Speedway than the Belond Equa-Flow, George Salih's 500-winning Epperly laydown.

Jud Phillips, meanwhile, was the stoic among roadster chiefs. Whenever things went impossibly wrong—and in Jud's racing they frequently seemed to—Jud knew how to put on a happy face and say, "Nothing's perfect!" which expressed the mixture of hopelessness, inevitability, and love he held for the impossible profession of chief. At Trenton for the New Jersey 100 of 1963, Jud wasn't overly perturbed when the clutch of his Leader Card 7 went out in morning warm-ups, even though replacing the clutch of a Watson roadster was an obnoxious job requiring the removal of the entire

Johnnie Pouelsen, standing, gives Parnelli Jones an earful in 1963, the year of their 500 win. "What I liked about John," Parnelli has said, "is that he always had the motto, 'I'll make it better. I'll make the race car run faster for you. We'll get this and that.' As a chief mechanic, he had the desire of a race driver." Which was hardly surprising. Just like the East Coast roadster chief Buster Warke, who did it for 35 years, Pouelsen was an ex-race driver of hot rod roadsters and sprint cars. *Bob Tronolone*

But you also heard stories about chief mechanics calling their drivers balloonfeet, strokers, and other derogatory names to manipulate them into going faster; chief mechanics putting their driver on the Brickyard practicing against opposition roadsters and ordering him not to return to the pits until he'd blown them all off; chief mechanics telling their driver, look, dummy, you've got the same chassis setup as Parnelli's, now go out there and run 150 miles per hour like he does. A. J. Watson worked with Buffer Red Flaherty, Troy Ruttman, Smokey Elisian, and, above, Rodger Ward. Asked, as the most successful Indy 500 chief of them all, what battle instructions he barked to his troops, the Head replied, "None. I didn't tell them anything. They all wanted to win. Worse than I did, probably." *Indy 500 Photos*

Meyer-Drake Offenhauser. With some assistance from the Head, who was there with the Kaiser Aluminum 1, Jud got the skeletonizing job completed in 20 minutes. But in spite of all this skilled crisis labor, Jud next got to observe his Leader Card 7 dropping dead after only 48 miles with a bad magneto; 5 miles later, Watson's own Kaiser Aluminum 1 was finished with a faulty fuel tank. Nothing's perfect!

What with all their creative problem-solving skills, and their self-reliance and obsession to make sacrifices for the sake of racing, all the dinosaur chiefs were unique bargains for the car owners who employed them. They were hugely underpaid and overworked. The top pay I ever heard a chief mechanic commanding in this era was the $10,000 that Smokey Yunick said he got paid for his services at the 1960 500, a race that brought him victory but no happiness, and that figure was ridiculously high compared to the norm. Dave Laycock, who served as chief of the Bill Forbes operation through four Indy 500s, received the magnificent annual "salary" of $20,000. But that was Laycock's whole seasonal operations budget; and Dave well understood that if he exhausted the $20,000 before a season was over, his patron Forbes—vice-president of Foster-Forbes Glass, a Chicago-area company bottling everything from beer to catsup—would shut everything down. Laycock, then, not only had to be thrifty with the 20 Gs, but had to regularly plow any and all prize money back into the running of the team. This he did with gusto.

Forbes and Laycock never had a signed agreement, only a spoken one. Forbes instructed Dave, "Every May first my race car is ready to run at Indianapolis or you don't have a job." And Laycock in 1962 went to ultra-obedient lengths satisfying the boss. At three o'clock in the afternoon of April 30, he put the Bill Forbes in line, then personally slept overnight in its cockpit making certain it was the first dinosaur onto the bricks when the Speedway opened officially at ten o'clock the next morning.

Jud Phillips, who from 1962 through 1965 fielded for Bob Wilke the Leader Card 7, the Leader Card 4, and the Wynn's Friction Proofing, managed to hold out for a 15-percent share of the prize money, in addition to a weekly wage of $150. Like most chiefs, Phillips was free to negotiate his own small sponsorship deals with contingency companies such as Perfect Circle, Monroe, and Autolite. All that still didn't add up to a lot of money, and so, to try and earn a little more, Jud fielded a sprint car team on dirt and high-bank short tracks during spare Friday and Saturday nights. A. J. Watson and a few of the other chiefs also often did this.

Making up for a chief mechanic's low income were a couple of wonderful compensations. For one thing, a chief could be fiercely independent and might tell the car owner to go screw himself if he felt like it. For another, the chief was free to run a seat-of-the-pants operation and to stamp his own identity and personality on it. When you thought about Leader Card, for example, you didn't so much identify the name with Bob Wilke as with Leader Card's two terrific chiefs, the Head and Jud Phillips. Similarly, you could almost say that Racing Associates wasn't really Ebb Rose's outfit at all but

Herb Porter's. Shirley Murphy might be the rich guy who was on the board of directors of the corporation that owned all the Sheraton hotels, and William Ansted might be the kingpin of Thompson Industries, a going concern that turned out zillions of automotive pieces for Dearborn and Detroit, but Sheraton-Thompson's captain was George Bignotti. J. C. Agajanian had his hog dynasty, but Johnnie Poulsen was the true force behind the Agajanian Willard Battery and the Agajanian Bowes Seal Fast. And Johnnie, that strange, strange dude, seemed to go out of the way annoying his master. Aggie always dressed to the hilt, so the chief mechanic perversely parodied his fashion-plate employer's elegant 10-gallon headdress with Johnnie's own crummy straw cowboy turban.

What a group! Every morning throughout May, emerging from the rows of wooden garages in Gasoline Alley where teams in the 500 were sheltered, you'd see the various chiefs and their slap-dash crews of stooges and gofers pushing or pulling their roadsters to their assigned spaces along the pit road. And they'd remain out there working and timing until dragging themselves and their roadsters back to their barns at six in the evening when the Speedway closed. Afterward they'd be out there relaxing and loitering on the cement and gravel spits in front of their respective garages. No longer having to yell to be heard above their own and the other Meyer-Drakes, the chiefs communicated in roadster nomenclature and cheerfully blasphemed back and forth because no members of the opposite sex were around to complain. And then, being social animals, most of them departed Gasoline Alley to end up all together again that night for more companionship and to toss a few at the White Front canteen, every chief's favorite gin mill.

You hadn't been to Indianapolis until you visited the White Front, or so the adage went.

Located out on 16th Street, just past the railroad trestle and cater-corner to the Speedway's first turn bleachers, the White Front from the outside was little but a grim concrete bunker surrounded by a moat of sharp lava rocks; and the architecture didn't get much better inside: just a few tables, stove, broken-down piano, and the bar. Nonetheless, every roadster evening during May the White Front was where chief mechanics celebrated the joy of being chief mechanics. And if you were a chief who was feeling poorly, you couldn't spend an hour at the White Front without leaving feeling better.

An unofficial tradition was that no White Front night could properly begin without the arrival of Jud Phillips. Like many chiefs, Jud was inward and nondemonstrative when he was racing. But he was big and bluff and with a few brews in him positively radiated good cheer. Thursdays were racing movie night, and Jud's improvised, uncensored narratives regularly brought down the White Front roof.

A fellow chief and White Front sovereign whom Jud sometimes got confused with because their names sounded similar, and because they'd both known interesting times being employed by Bruce Homeyer, was Rocky Philipp. Rocky's personal legend at the White Front had begun on the night and early morning after a

Hoosier Hundred at the Indianapolis Fairgrounds across town. The champ dirt car for which Rocky had been chief mechanic had done well, taking second, and after paying off its driver, Rocky had $2,600 left. Knowing what celebrations at the White Front could be like, Rocky asked the management if he could deposit the money overnight in the safe in the basement.

And in the predawn hours after the White Front closed, somebody broke in and removed the safe and Rocky's $2,600. Easy come, easy go. By coincidence, the White Front next announced plans to regroom its old potholed parking lot and treat it to an extensive coat of fresh asphalt. Forever afterward, the newly paved strip was known as "Rocky's Parking Lot."

Dave Laycock, one of the few chiefs who actually lived in Indianapolis, was the brat of the White Front. Compared to the White Front's more grizzled faces, Laycock looked too young to be guzzling beer, and he almost was. First breaking into racing by hawking newspapers and programs out at the Speedway when he was 9 or 10, Laycock by the age of 17 was a $50-a-week-gofer for Herb Porter and at 21 became a full-blown chief for Bill Forbes.

Dave was a bachelor, but the White Front wasn't a singles bar. Women weren't absolutely outlawed from coming in, but their patronage was discouraged because most chief mechanics believed it impossible to discuss racing and drink peaceably in their presence. Not, of course, that life in the White Front was necessarily peaceful, and especially not when Laycock's former boss Herb Porter was on the rampage.

Everybody liked Herb when he was sober, but nobody much liked him when he drank himself into oblivion, lost his temper, and tried sucker-punching somebody. Usually the danger signal was when Herb removed his dentures and passed them to somebody like Laycock to take care of.

Away from the White Front, Herb was the official chief mechanic's representative on the directors' board of the U.S. Auto Club. He went clear back to the pioneer roadster period of the Rich Kids, Vookie, and the Fuel Injection Special, and he considered himself not simply a chief, but more like an engineer and innovator. He had a great way with words. "My biggest fuckin' problem," he once said, "is that I've been around the Speedway too fuckin' long, and been a student of the 500 too fuckin' long, and what pisses me off is listening to dumb bastards telling me fuckin' things I know are fuckin' wrong when I got more data on this fuckin' place than anybody else." Sometimes Herb's whole life seemed to be dedicated to receiving credit for all the things he claimed to have done.

Famous fist fights occasionally got fought out on Rocky's Parking Lot in response to some of Herb's claims, but, as far as I can determine, Herb was legitimately entitled to crow the way he did. He really was good, and hearing Indy 500 neophytes "taking credit for inventing the fuckin' wheel" quite understandably inflamed him. In fairness to Herb, most of the other dinosaur chiefs were similarly suspicious of anybody not of the immediate family. Maybe they didn't talk about it as loudly as Herb, but they, too, knew how

good they were at their work, and knew who deserved honor at the Speedway and White Front and who did not. Indeed, being chief of a dinosaur roadster at Indy in the fifties and sixties was like being in an unofficial but exclusive fraternity.

Respect, then, was important—especially to Herb Porter. Lots of acclaim and even money went to whatever chief mechanic won the 500 every year, but acclaim was less important than the respect and acceptance of the existing chief mechanic fraternity. Herb never tolerated outsiders. "We used to get into some, well, TOUGH debates," Herb once told me. "And some of us refused to be intimidated. And finally you heard all you wanted. So you PUNCHED the son-of-a-bitch." Almost but not quite managing to sound apologetic, he hastily added, "I wasn't the only one."

He certainly wasn't. Yet Herb did succeed in embroiling himself in what was the most spectacular, and shortest, exchange of opinions ever to involve a pair of dinosaur chiefs.

It didn't actually occur in the White Front at all, but a few blocks up the street inside the bar on the first floor of the Holiday Inn that faced the Speedway across 16th Street. The hostilities kicked off while Herb was seated at a table becoming tanked and rapidly making himself choleric, "debating" a visitor named Fran Hernandez about how fuel injection worked. Hernandez was a technician for Autolite spark plugs, a sharp Chicano who'd rigged up hot rods for the southern California dry lakes and V-8-60 Ford midgets at Gilmore Stadium. But it didn't matter. To Herb, Hernandez was nothing but an outsider who wasn't part of the dinosaur chief mechanic circle, just another know-nothing late-comer of a motor mouth.

So, wearying of all the drivel he was having to listen to, Herb predictably lost his temper and whaled on Fran Hernandez with a thundering haymaker. Two things marking the occasion as different from others were (1) Herb surprised one and all by not first removing his dentures, and (2) this time one of his Sunday punches had actually landed. Fran went toppling backwards off his chair, then fled.

Herb, according to witnesses, was so elated about at last really connecting that he'd decided to go hand out a second. He went hunting for Fran and at last found him again in the Holiday's other bar on the second story.

Another study of the king of the roadsters, the wondrous Sheraton-Thompson 1 of the previous chapter. In preparation for the campaign of 1964, George Bignotti delivered it to Kuzma's L.A. emporium and gave Eddie Ka-zoom a list of improvements to implement. They included moving the seat back to make A. J. Foyt more comfortable in the cockpit, re-positioning the fuel tank to place more weight on the rear tires, adjusting the placements of the radius rods, and adding a ram-air hood scoop and later a bleed strip. "All very minor stuff," George said, "but when you add four or five minor things to a race car, all of a sudden it's better." "Better" is putting it mildly. The Sheraton-Thompson earned the most seasonal prize money of any dinosaur, better than $180,000 in 1964 dollars. And it was responsible for making Foyt the national driving champion for a fourth time. *Indy 500 Photos*

Other roadster personalities and chiefs also happened to be up there playing lounge lizards, and one of them was Chickie Hirashima. Chickie must have been as startled as everyone else when Herb came bursting into the bar all gassed and making for Hernandez with his fist cocked and uttering comments about Mexicans. Noticing Chickie, he uttered for good measure a few about the Japanese.

Now, in World War II Chickie had first passed a miserable year and a day with his family as interns of the detention gulag of Manzanar in the frozen High Sierra. Following that, he'd been one of the earliest volunteers for the all-Japanese 442nd, the high-risk combat squad whose members got terribly shot up in Sicily at the Battle of Anzio, then fought across the mountains of Italy and France, blowing away Nazis clear into Germany. Chickie, in other words, took slurs seriously, which was why Herb ended up having a bar stool brought down on his head. By Chickie. It was a real puzzler, because Herb was 6 feet tall and nobody could quite work out

On the surface, the collaboration between a chief mechanic and a race driver was a story of two men compensating for what each was lacking: the chief's inability to race the car, the driver's inability to work on it. It should have been a happy deal for all concerned. Chiefs and drivers alike enjoyed what they did, and both lived to see their race car leading and winning. Guess again, though. Notwithstanding all their successes, George and A. J. made one another miserable. *Bob Tronolone*

how the 5 foot 2 inch Chickie had reached him. But everybody at the Holiday apparently approved, because after Herb crumpled to the floor everybody left him lying there to wake up on his own.

During a long-running conversation I had with Herb in 1994, he told me he'd been off the sauce for the last 30 years, yet still was fuzzy about the events that night at the Holiday. "Chickie crowned me with a chair," he said. "I don't know what happened." It seemed to settle the score, though. Again sounding almost—but not quite—apologetic, he went on, "Chickie and I always were good friends and still were to the day Chickie died." Voice raising, and in his own defense, Herb snapped, "But goddamnit! When you get enough bourbon in you . . ."

*I*n the 1961 Indy, when Rodger Ward began hearing a vibration in his Leader Card 2 and terminated his fight for the lead to come onto pit road whining for A. J. Watson to fix the vibration right in the

For 500 after 500, Clint Brawner, chief of frugal Dean Van Lines, got away with running the same piston rings, rod bearings, and even gaskets as many as eight 500s' old. Wally Meskowski was another veteran chief who could do a lot with a little. Chief of the Bryant Heating & Cooling 9 in 1963, Wally had just one Offenhauser to get him through all the miles of practicing, time trials, and the 500 itself. The work load was too heavy, and during practice the Bryant burned out a piston, forcing Wally to stay up all night repairing and rebuilding and afterward crossing his fingers that his patch job could survive time trials and the 500. Well, the Bryant subsequently qualified tenth fastest. And almost all Memorial Day long it was in the middle of a series of rocketing battles for second and third and occasionally the lead. *Indy 500 Photos*

middle of the 500, the Head for once blew his cool and bellowed at Ward: "Get back out there and race, you jerk! What do you think I am, the guy at the corner gas station?" That's precisely what a chief was—a problem-solver and jack-of-all-trades just as up on the chemistry and inner workings of an Offy roadster as a mechanic at a small filling station was up on the idiosyncrasies of his customers' heaps. Only its chief really knew how to work on a dinosaur and make it go fast. Excepting perhaps Jack Zink, no car owner could have operated the team minus the services of its chief.

Even so, a dinosaur chief mechanic lived in a state of anxiety knowing that he could lose his job and status inside Gasoline Alley and the White Front in an instant. All that had to happen was for a car owner and a chief to get sideways with each other. Or for a car owner to run out of money and put the chief mechanic on ice by allowing the team to go belly-up.

For ten of the dozen dinosaur seasons relations between car owners and chiefs remained copacetic in the main. And then, for roughly six months between 1962 and 1963, a sudden eruption of firings and resignations and bad mojo involving nine teams and five dinosaur roadsters completely rearranged the careers of seven chiefs, including three of the heavyweights: George Bignotti, Jud Phillips, and Rocky Philipp.

George

Indianapolis, 1962, was probably where it all began. And what happened there was that—to the surprise of nobody who knew anything about their already explosive history together—George Bignotti and his national champion driver, A. J. Foyt, who'd won the 500 together the previous year with the Bowes Seal Fast 1, decided that it was totally impossible for them to get along anymore.

Next to A. J. Watson himself, George Bignotti probably carried the most mystique of any dinosaur chief. But it was a different kind of mystique. Whether inside Gasoline Alley or at the White Front, the Head was openly cordial, always his casual self. George, on the other hand, was seldom automatically friendly and was rarely seen in the White Front at all.

The twin goals of A. J. and most chiefs was to win all the races; they hated seeing their race cars get outrun, they had a race driver's mentality that way—and to earn a small buck enjoying the roadster life. George seemed to aim higher than that—to use racing as a means of advancing himself. George sought fame. More than being

merely a chief mechanic, he was a car owner himself, partners with Bob Bowes in the Bowes Seal Fast team. As the Bowes driver, A. J. Foyt received 40 percent of all prize money; Bignotti and Bowes plowed 50 percent of what remained into team upkeep; and all the Bowes Seal Fast stooges and gofers got the remaining 10 percent plus a bonus if they worked all season.

Like so many of his peers, Bignotti hailed from California, but not L.A. Bignotti was from the San Francisco Bay area. His boyhood was typical, being race cars, race cars, all the way, except for an unexpected stint as a florist. Even when he was in high school enrolling in classes teaching machine shop and mechanical drawing, George seemed to be planning ahead, because such schooling enabled him to construct and race his own midget Offys four and five nights a week around the City by the Bay. By 1956, he was at Indy with a lightweight upright roadster, the Bowes Seal Fast 15, built to George's personal specs by Kurtis-Kraft.

Nothing came out of this particular Bignotti roadster, even though George now thinks it was probably ahead of its time. By 1959 George was ready to quit racing. Within months of each other he had two drivers killed and two dinosaurs destroyed, one of them the old Bowes Seal Fast 15; the vocation of florist was looking very good again. But then Floyd Trevis built Bignotti the Bowes Seal Fast 1, the upright that made itself the most successful of all Watson look-alikes and that won George and A. J. Foyt the stirring 1961 Indy. Seldom was a chief mechanic's cool adaptability in a crisis put to a sterner test. A fueling apparatus malfunctioned on the last pit stop, and the Bowes Seal Fast 1 had re-entered the 500 leading but without enough methanol to finish. Not a man to panic, or to concede defeat, George borrowed the storage tank and fueling nozzle off Chickie Hirashima's Leader Card 41, which had fallen out of the 500 earlier. And then George signaled Foyt back into the pits for the Bowes Seal Fast 1's famous, and winning, stop-and-go fuel splash.

Afterward, Indianapolis and championship racing generally entered a period when nobody mentioned George's name without including that of Foyt. They won so often that they were supposed to be the dinosaur era's "super team"—but only during a race. When they weren't racing, it was something else. I'm not sure which version is the correct one, but in the course of my research for this book I had somebody in the know describe George as an old-fashioned bully who needled A. J. relentlessly. And then I had another prominent party describe George as a weak pushover who

Among many contenders, arguably the most frequently wrecked of all roadsters was the Bell Lines Trucking, a 1962 Watson that competed in two Indy 500s, once on a southern super-speedway, and 18 times on miles like Trenton and Milwaukee. At Milwaukee in the 1962 summer it absorbed a huge pasting that put it out of commission for nearly a year, and at Trenton in the 1964 spring it got smacked from behind and completely up-ended. It was repaired again and three weeks afterwards, here at Indianapolis, it qualified 18th fastest. During the 500 it was storming to the front until flattening a tire and skidding across the infield. At the Atlanta 300 of 1966, now called the Dayton Steel Wheel, it collected its last bruise. Arriving back in the pits after finishing a hot fifth, the old roadster was getting serenaded so enthusiastically by its mechanics for its especially fine job of smoking off the Dayton team's own funny car, that the Dayton Steel Wheel's driver became overexcited: seeing the funny car parked there, he gave it a playful nudge in the butt. The funny car stood firm, but the nudge folded up and buckled the Dayton Steel Wheel's own fiberglass nose. *Indy 500 Photos*

somewhat taught himself to ignore all the terrible things Foyt called him when A. J. was angry. Either way, George and A. J. made a maddening team.

Differences notwithstanding, the two managed to win the 1962 opener at Trenton. But in Indianapolis throughout May gossip inside the White Front had A. J. purposely trying to annoy George every way he could think of. First he seemed to challenge George's authority with the addition of his, A. J.'s, father as a sort of co-chief. And then Foyt went out to Indianapolis Raceway Park and won a nickel-and-dime sprint car meet, scorning Bignotti's request that he not risk his neck racing on the eve of the 500.

Winner of Indy the previous year, the Bowes Seal Fast operation was struggling all month. Throughout warm-ups and time trials, dinosaurs like the Bill Forbes, the Agajanian Willard Battery, and the Leader Card 3 were all nudging 150, but Foyt and the Bowes Seal Fast could not. They couldn't even qualify on the front row. Worse, just the afternoon before the 500, there was panic in the Bowes garage. According to George, while the Bowes Seal Fast roadster was in the middle of final prep, some lock-tight gum got inside its injectors, and everybody in the crew was up most of the night cleaning it out. Not until the following morning's 500 would anybody remember that in all the haste and confusion somebody neglected to secure a brake pedal cotter key.

Right when A. J. was in the middle of a refueling and rubber stop at 160 miles, the offending cotter key popped loose and let the brake pedal of the Bowes Seal Fast go to the floor. Having just taken the lead courtesy of the pace-setting Agajanian Willard Battery's own pit stop, A. J. wasn't delighted to hear George asking him to shut down the engine and drag himself out of the wheelhouse so a crew member could burrow inside the cockpit with a new cotter key and repair the brakes.

The repairs went slowly. The Bowes Seal Fast fell a lap behind. Even with the new cotter key in place, and A. J. back in the cockpit and the refueling complete, one of the tire changers was late. A. J. went ballistic. Then the tire changer, freaking out at all the screaming, forgot to hammer the knock-off tight. And just as the Bowes Seal Fast arrived in the first turn, the wheel fell off.

There was a violent swerve followed by a big veer, but the Bowes didn't hit anything and A. J. wasn't hurt. Storming back to the pits

Jud "Nothing's Perfect!" Phillips. The emblem of the White Front, he waited a decade or more for his first championship win as a chief, but it was a big one, followed immediately by a second. *Bob Tronolone*

on foot, he still wasn't through racing and commandeered another dinosaur, the Sarkes-Tarzian. It had already helped set off a four-roadster wreck and worn out its assigned driver as well as one relief pilot. A. J. jumped in anyway, then bailed out just as fast when an alcohol fire flashed through the cockpit and put the zap on his posterior.

A. J. and George figuratively gritted their teeth and regrouped. Ten days later the Bowes Seal Fast won a mad race at Milwaukee. But Foyt and Bignotti still found working together to be a royal pain. That July they won their third meet of the campaign, a match at Langhorne on dirt, but three weeks afterward at Trenton when the same Langhorne-winning Bowes vehicle began malfunctioning and oiling, the Bowes Seal Fast team at last flatlined with A. J. walking out and telling George to go to hell.

George went instead to Bobby Marshman, a past Indy rookie of the year and a go-getter. Bobby had gotten Shirley Murphy and William Ansted—two owners who were among the dinosaur era's freest-spending—to erect a powerful new Sheraton-Thompson team with George its chief mechanic, Bobby its trigger, and the 1961 Indy-winning Bowes Seal Fast 1 the bullet. Yet Marshman never got to win a race with George because Murphy and Ansted soon had second thoughts. Per George, the two owners came to the conclusion that the driver they truly coveted wasn't Bobby Marshman after all. It was A. J.

Having already taken Marshman to six races that 1962 summer without winning one, George told Murphy and Ansted, sure, he was prepared to try again with A. J. And A. J. was more than eager to reunite with George. Following their break, Foyt had gotten star employment on the Indy squad of Lindsey Hopkins, who'd pink-slipped Don Branson to make room for him. But life on the Hopkins team hadn't been what he'd hoped for, and now A. J., who'd won nothing for three months, was desperate to bail out and regroup. He'd additionally suffered the largest humiliation of his career, ever, when he'd gotten fired out of his sprint car ride, the Konstant Hot Special, by a mouthy stooge named Carl Nosal.

So A. J. and Bobby Marshman agreed, in effect, to play racing musical chairs. A. J. quit Lindsey Hopkins to come to Sheraton-Thompson, and after Murphy and Ansted agreed to pay Marshman a $5,000 bonus if he'd go away, Bobby joined Hopkins.

AL KELLER & CREW · 1961 · INDIANAPOLIS MOTOR SPEEDWAY

Jud, second from the left, puts three bodies between himself and his difficult employer and Konstant Hot car owner, Bruce Homeyer, far right. To Bruce's left is super-stooge Carl Nosal. *Indy 500 Photos*

Reviving their old love-hate relationship at Sacramento that October, George and Foyt won. Then in 1964 they proceeded to win just about every other pavement or dirt championship contest worth winning, including Indy.

Enough was enough, though. They remained together through two and a half seasons—all they could stand of each other—and then George and A. J. had yet another acrimonious blow-up in the middle of 1965, right after the dinosaur era had finished. This one stuck.

Jud

At roughly the same time that Bignotti and Foyt were parting for the first time in 1962, Jud Phillips, too, was finding himself in perilous conditions.

Going inside Gasoline Alley and wandering from roadster team to roadster team, and chief mechanic to chief mechanic, you found that each had a different identity and feel. Sheraton-Thompson and George Bignotti, say, had lots of money as well as Bignotti's intimidating knowledge and ambition. Leader Card and A. J. Watson had money as well as Watson's own cool smarts and intimacy with his products; as Hank Blum said, sometimes the Head seemed able to make one of the Leader Card Watsons run faster just by giving it a kick.

And Jud ("Nothing's Perfect!") Phillips, even during his rotten stay of a season and a half with Konstant Hot and boozy Bruce Homeyer, was always a chief mechanic who exuded a gruff good cheer, whether he meant it or not.

Throughout roadster Indy, Jud was always one of the best. Born in Los Angeles, he had a brainy brother who won a scholarship to the University of Southern California, a mother who was a grade school teacher, and a father who was a pencil pusher for Los Angeles County—a career bureaucrat who led a secure and risk-free life. That was the exact opposite of the existence Jud picked for himself.

Just like almost everyone in the community of chiefs, Jud grew up working on cars. He was working on one out in the garage of his parents' home the morning of Pearl Harbor. Drafted into World War II at 18, he was shipped to deep Texas for training in the infantry. Then, when the armistice was only two months away, he was processed back to L.A. on a troop train. But all orders changed, and the next thing to happen was that the train backed up and switched directions for New Jersey—Jud and the other dog faces were getting floated to Le Havre, France, for two years. Nothing's perfect!

Uncle Sam made Jud a sergeant in the motor pool, and he learned lots about the inner workings of military vehicles. Home again, he bored straight into racing.

Everybody in the L.A. scene of the forties and fifties was a lunatic for racing of one variety or another—hot rods, midgets, sprints, stocks, and of course, Indy—and the namesake of the dealership where Jud was working, Bob Estes Lincoln-Mercury, was one of the biggest lunatics. Estes had glorious intentions and pitifully low funds—Indy's time-honored recipe for frustration. In 1951, Jud and A. J. Watson were the green but rough-and-ready co-chiefs of an Estes econo lump at the 500. Struggling, making miracles with a medley of worn and junk parts, at last they got it in the show. When the driveshaft popped after eight laps, the month of endless labor ended with the heap finishing 33rd and abysmally last.

His apprenticeship completed, Jud couldn't wait to do it all over again, and did, chiefing hapless Estes Lincoln-Mercury dinosaurs through all the Indy 500s of the fifties. His "Nothing's perfect!" adventures were alarming: accidents, even disasters and deaths—Jud married the widow of one of his drivers—and the closer Jud came to achieving his first win as a chief at Indy or anywhere, the more it seemed to tease and elude him.

In 1961, losing heart at last, Bob Estes decided that nine unsuccessful tries at winning Indianapolis were enough and put his team on the market. To the great complication of Jud's life, Bruce Homeyer purchased everything.

What with all the revenue from his miniature water heaters and other hardware, Homeyer had deeper pockets and bigger bucks to fling at Indy than well-meaning Estes and his dinky dealership ever had. And Homeyer did proceed to spend lots of Konstant Hot money. But Homeyer had his other hobby, his drinking hobby. Whacking the fire water made him prone to throw his weight around and begin reading the riot act to Jud, who wouldn't take it.

Jud and Bruce fought about everything. Bruce wanted Jud to relocate from L.A. to the Konstant Hot home in New Jersey, and they fought about that. Besides the dinosaur roadster work Jud already performed, Bruce wanted Jud working on the Konstant Hot midget Offys, and they fought about that, because Jud had never lost his L.A. hot-rodder's intolerance for doodlebugs. Bruce didn't like the chauffeurs Jud put in the Konstant Hot dinosaur and sprint car, and they really fought over that, their ideas of what a race driver should be like being radically opposite.

Jud's idea of a really top pedal man was Don Branson. Merely getting through Indy's 500 miles could be a cruel ordeal for Branson because he had chronic low blood pressure and generally looked so wasted and geriatric he appeared older than his 40-plus years. Don was a grump to boot. Nevertheless, as long as he didn't get pooped out he was inferior to no one. Along with Rodger Ward and Shorty Templeman, the two other senior citizen roadster pilots, old Branson was poison to all the young hot dogs.

But Bruce Homeyer, too, had strong preferences. He dug wild men drivers like Jack ("Upside-Down") Rounds, and Al Keller, the crash-hound half-breed Cherokee known as "the Dirty Indian," who had lost a thumb at Langhorne in 1955 and later that season at Indy had sped up to join the Vukovich backstraight wreck.

Every chief in the White Front minded every other chief's business, so Jud was on the receiving end of much sympathy, free beers, and unsolicited advice on how to hang in there and outlast his maniac of a car owner. Throughout, Jud wore his "Nothing's perfect!" expression.

"Never forget that I'm the boss," Bruce would lecture. "But you don't know anything," Jud would reply.

Jud could get away with being insubordinate because Bruce would have had a hell of a time replacing him, and knew it. He'd never won the 500, true, but after better than a decade at Indy and the White Front, Jud's reputation was the best. With his casual but hip L.A. persona, Jud—perhaps more than any other chief—must have been the one some of the Hoosiers had in mind when they invented the insult/compliment, TMC, "Too Much California." Solid as his reputation as a chief was, Jud, when he chose to practice the craft, was almost equally esteemed as a race car builder. Though scarcely the equivalent of A. J. Watson cranking out his 23 roadsters at 421 West Palmer, Jud, too, had personally constructed some fast dinosaurs and sprint cars. Homeyer well knew this. Bruce, in fact, had been pressuring Jud to build some new Konstant Hot iron and Jud had always made up excuses why he couldn't.

By the end of 1961, though, all Jud's excuses had run out. Upside-Down had violently overturned a Konstant Hot sprinter at Reading, and Konstant Hot's dirt champ rig had gotten mangled during the Dirty Indian's fatal accident at Phoenix. So Homeyer's team was in desperate need of replacements. Jud outdid himself. For 1962, he built Bruce a duplicate of a Watson roadster as well as an amazing sprint car. Armed with megaphone exhausts, a honking Traco V-8, and perfect four-torsion-bar suspension, and resplendent in the jet black and gold leaf livery of Konstant Hot, it was drop-dead beautiful.

Jud had originally tapped Don Branson as its driver, but Bruce overruled him. He made Jud fire Branson to make room

The magnificent geezer Don Branson. *Bob Tronolone*

for A. J. Foyt, who was in the middle of his big battle with George Bignotti, and who had already treated the new Konstant Hot sprint car to a win at Indianapolis Raceway Park in May. Yet by July, two months later, matters still remained up in the air at Konstant Hot. Homeyer had had different drivers in and out of all his equipment, always unsuccessfully. Bruce was on the warpath and was planning to make more trouble by coming to the next championship race at Langhorne.

So Langhorne's water-logged infield parking lot became Bruce's and Jud's Gun Fight at the OK Corral. The meet had rained out and gotten postponed, and all the chief mechanics had finished loading up and were departing. And Jud was concluding plans to spend the week's layover drinking beer and going fishing with Jim Hurtubise and his brother and father on their family island up in Canada. Then Bruce Homeyer arrived.

Jud knew it was going to be dangerous. By this time of the day Bruce was always three-quarters bombed and mean-drunk.

"Where do you think you're going?" Bruce asked.

"Canada," Jud replied.

"No, no," Bruce protested. "I'm still the boss. You're coming to New Jersey to work on my midgets."

"Never the midgets," Jud said.

"Well, if you're not going to work on the midgets you can't work on any of my stuff," Bruce said.

The chief mechanic's book on lead-foot Roger McCluskey was that if he could keep from sticking his head up his posterior, he could win the 500. In 1963 he came close. Close, but no cigar. *Bob Tronolone*

Previous pages: Branson's Leader Card 4, 500 winner in 1962, paid a 1963 visit to the wall after first skidding 774 feet. Don then qualified it on the front row at better than 150 miles per hour. And after an emergency pit stop with five miles to go, he came in fifth. *Bob Tronolone*

"OK," Jud said.

Following his week in Canada with the Hurtubise clan, Jud returned to Indianapolis where many of the dinosaur teams headquartered year-round. Times were hard that summer of 1962. Not only had Jud lost his job at Konstant Hot, but Foyt and Bignotti were in the middle of their split, Bell Lines Trucking was in disarray, Bill Forbes was changing drivers, and so on. But Jud succeeded in discovering something temporary with Leader Card and Bob Wilke.

It wasn't a racing assignment, strictly a crash repair gig. A. J. Watson had won Wilke a second Indy 500 that May with the Leader Card 3, but the upstart personnel behind the Leader Card 7 who had collaborated to give Wilke a smashing one-two finish were among the missing. The Leader Card 7's temporary chief, Chickie Hirashima, had gone back to L.A. The Leader Card 7's driver, Len Sutton, was home in Portland, Oregon, recuperating from serious back wounds after wrecking just one week after the 500 at Milwaukee. And the Leader Card 7 itself—it was the former Leader Card 41, one of the two freak coil-over Watsons from the previous year—was still all beat to junk after Sutton's spill.

Watson was too busy with his own Leader Card 3, so Wilke asked Jud to repair it. And at the same time Wilke wondered if Jud might be able to do something with Leader Card's troublesome backup championship dirt car, which had had a severe case of wheel-hop ever since Jimmy Bryan's accident of two seasons prior.

With the assistance of "Einstein," a stooge who deviled for a lot of teams in Gasoline Alley, Jud got the Leader Card 7 shipshape again. And he developed some ideas about how to cure the wheel-hop of Wilke's dirt champ car. Then Wilke said, "Why don't I just give you the two cars for a few races and you find somebody to drive them?"

As ever, Don Branson was Jud's top candidate. But when Jud found him, the old man was grumpier than ever. And with ample reason. Following his humiliating dismissal by Bruce Homeyer, Don had been bouncing from team to team, angrily trying to run over black-and-gold Konstant Hot Equipment whenever he saw it on the track ahead of him. And he was also seething about A. J. Foyt. Not only had Foyt first taken Don's Konstant Hot sprint car ride away from him, but Foyt, following his break with Bignotti, had reportedly next gone and bad-mouthed Branson to Lindsey Hopkins and taken away Don's Indy dinosaur ride as well! Now Don was out of a ride for a third time. Having just the previous Sunday at the Milwaukee 200 replaced Roger McCluskey as the chauffeur of the Bell Lines Trucking, Don had gotten caught in the middle of a multi-roadster wreck not of his making. As a result, the Bell Lines Trucking had suffered major damage, and now Bell Lines was folding its whole dinosaur operation.

Jud told Don that he had this Watson, the Leader Card 7, that he was going to be chief mechanic of: "Would you like to drive it?"

As a matter of fact, Don didn't, not much. Unlike younger drivers, Branson was an old-school veteran who disliked Watsons—pretty much disliked offset roadsters generally—and still much preferred a top-heavy dirt champ car so he could sit bolt upright with the driveshaft spinning and flailing right under his posterior.

Jud explained to him he had a Leader Card dirt car as well, and that got Don's interest. Langhorne, the track where Jud had parted company with Bruce Homeyer just three races and five months earlier, was holding a second 1962 race that Sunday. It became Jud's and Don's Leader Card debut.

Don won. Actually, it was more like a three-way triumph: Branson got his first win as an Indy car driver; Jud got his first as a chief; and Leader Card got its first and only score at Langhorne. Not that it was easy. Branson took so much dirt in the face from all the cars he was lapping that he finished the 100 miles half-blind. He won at record speed anyway, then had to spend the night in an infirmary getting his eyes cleaned out.

A little later at Trenton, Don was a regenerated but still grumpy grandpop anxiously leaning forward in the wheelhouse and careening into corners so hot that for 200 searing miles everything was tilting over violently—dirt car, tall tires, and naturally Don himself. Scaring all the roadsters silly, Branson and Jud and Leader Card won again.

And from then until the close of the dinosaur era, Jud and Branson could do no wrong. Bob Wilke took them on full time as Leader Card's second team, and Branson even condescended to get out of the dirt car and occasionally be railroaded into the reclining cockpit of a Watson roadster. Don never much liked doing it, though, not even on March 28, 1965, when he and the Wynn's Friction Proofing won the 150-miler at Phoenix International Raceway. Having the final roadster victory go to the race driver who always disliked all roadsters amounted to another of Jud's "Nothing's perfect!" deals.

Meanwhile, for the rest of his own days, Jud never could decide whether Bruce Homeyer had fired him that day at Langhorne, or he'd quit.

Rocky

Rocky Philipp would follow Jud as chief mechanic for Homeyer's outfit, spicing up a Konstant Hot Watson for driver Roger McCluskey. Yet Homeyer wasn't solely responsible for teaming up Philipp and McCluskey. The credit goes in part to one Carl Nosal, who opened up a spot for McCluskey by ousting none other than A. J. Foyt. And in the 1963 500, Rocky almost put McCluskey into the winner's circle. But not quite.

When Jud Phillips and Bruce Homeyer used to be having at it, Jud would tell Bruce what a chintzy and demanding employer Homeyer was for making Jud toil on three different race cars all by himself with only the erratic assistance of "a fat stooge."

That stooge happened to be Carl Nosal, all 5-foot-9-inch, 250 pounds of him. A vocal, good-natured gofer who was employed at the Konstant Hot plant in New Jersey when he wasn't assisting Jud at Indianapolis or out on the championship tour, Nosal had once gained a type of fame at the White Front. During a rare "Ladies Night," Carl won the dance contest performing the Twist.

Nosal was present at Langhorne the day Jud and Bruce had their last fight; afterward, Homeyer placed Carl in charge of the Konstant Hot sprint car, the luscious one Jud had built, with A. J. Foyt continuing to race it. So much authority went to Carl's head.

One day Homeyer telephoned to ask how things were going with Foyt.

"I fired him," Carl replied.

"You what?!" shouted Homeyer.

"He was jerking me around," answered Carl. "Don't worry."

So a fresh driver had to be found to race Konstant Hot's sprinter, dirt champ car, and dinosaur. This was when Homeyer brought in Roger McCluskey.

Word has come down that roadster drivers were tough guys who comported themselves with a we-are-risking-our-lives solemnity, and who postured about the Speedway with their chests thrown out telling everyone how brave they were. McCluskey was nothing like that. His personality and reputation were made the night that he did something that had all the hard drinkers of the White Front laughing for a week. This was in 1961. Chief steward Harlan Fengler couldn't resist giving cowed rookie drivers like McCluskey the treatment, and it seemed that Fengler had been ripping Roger up for Roger having veered inside the white stripe while lining up his dinosaur for turn 1. Wrapping up what had been a lengthy harangue, Fengler lectured Roger to never do that "except in an emergency." There was a moment of strained silence, broken by Roger's trademark giggle. "Uh, well, Harlan? *Every* time I go into turn 1 is an emergency!"

An impudent driver who in those circumstances could put down a figure of authority as well as ridicule his own driving, clearly was a valuable addition to dinosaur Indianapolis if only for his wit and humor. And so Roger proved to be. Curiously enough, in addition to being a funny man, Roger, in the manner of Jud Phillips, was a deep-rooted pessimist: If anything bad was ever going to happen, he figured it was going to happen to him. Still, he couldn't resist laughing and making everybody around him laugh.

Roger, however, hadn't been joking with Harlan Fengler about Indy's turn 1. He really did dislike it, just as he disliked almost everything else about the Speedway, except the prize money. Roger had come to Indy out of Arizona and southern California sprint cars. He was one of the fastest short-track racers, and savage 30-lap main events lasting just 15 miles seemed perfect for him. In comparison, when trying to complete the 500 miles of Indy, he invariably had his head up his butt. In 1961 he was in a Dennie Moore lowbelly laydown and got into a six-roadster crash right on the front straightaway; in 1962 he overshot the pits and later spun out the Bell Lines Trucking Watson; and in 1963 he was to have yet another prickly emergency with a Konstant Hot Watson.

But that was a ways in the future. In the summer of 1962, Roger wasn't making any money racing dinosaurs, as usual, so he badly needed a strong sprint car ride. Konstant Hot was supposed to have the best. And sure enough, despite the late start, with Roger racing

it and Carl Nosal maintaining it, the Konstant Hot nearly won the national splinter title.

Nice going. Bruce Homeyer, feeling that his new driver deserved a nice Christmas present, ordered Roger a new Watson roadster for the 1963 500. As an added gift, Bruce hired Roger an esteemed chief mechanic. It was Rocky Philipp, of "Rocky's Parking Lot" White Front fame.

"Rocky" was formidably burly and well tattooed, and hardly anybody ever called him by his real name, Bob. His nickname suggested that he might be a hard case who enjoyed beating people up, but even though in his racing he was frequently aligned with individuals who relished throwing blows—Herb Porter, for one—Rocky abhorred fisticuffs. His nickname, in fact, was meant to be ironic. It was another White Front story. Back when he was still known as "Bob," Rocky had stumbled inside the White Front one evening all punched-out and generally looking like he'd been clapped over the head by a bag of rocks. Rocky always refused to explain what had happened, but the favored account was that he'd had a job done on him by a jealous husband. Like many dinosaur chiefs, he was reputed to be a secret ladies' man.

Born in northern Michigan, he'd first gotten into racing with midget cars. But the Michigan winters froze Rocky's bones and he fled West for the sun and smog of L.A. of the dinosaur fifties, when the city was more Indianapolis than Indianapolis. For a man who went out of his way avoiding trouble and violence, Rocky found lots of it. One of his best racing pals, for instance, was Bob Pankratz, a tin man whose reputation as a brilliant flake even exceeded that of A. J. Watson's Fat Boy, Wayne Ewing. Pankratz and Rocky were chatting with Hart Fullerton, an automobile dealer who owned a roadster team, when Pankratz heard Fullerton's own bodyman hammering out a tail and went over to critique his work. The other bodyman took offense and swung on Pankratz. Pankratz swung back, and a melee broke out in front of Rocky's anguished eyes.

At Indy in 1958, Rocky managed to get appointed chief mechanic for one of the most ornery and penny-pinching owners, Norm Demler. It was a personality mismatch the equal of Jud Phillips and Bruce Homeyer. Demler treated Rocky like chattel; wouldn't even allow Rocky to pay any stooges to help him. Then the car owner started withholding food, forcing Rocky to forage around Gasoline Alley hoping that other chiefs might notice him, take pity, and invite him inside their garages to give him something to eat.

Demler's dinosaur was an Epperly lowbelly laydown, one Rocky had many problems making work, and George Amick, the vehicle's lead-foot rookie pilot, could only qualify on the ninth row. Because Demler continued to withhold funds, Rocky had additional problems hiring race day personnel. He wasn't sure what to do. Finally, around midnight on the morning of the 500, he sized up the White Front's floating population of disenfranchised chiefs, stooges, bumped drivers and the ilk, then sobered up and recruited a motley pit crew.

The 1958 500 had the heart torn out of it by the accident of the three Watsons on the first lap, followed by the mass elimination of many of the upright Kurtis-Krafts. Yet several of the laydowns maneuvered safely through the debris, including Rocky's Demler, which Amick floorboarded to second place. It was a good payday for Rocky, or would have been, except that Demler now accused the chief mechanic and his slapdash White Front crew of blowing a possible victory with their disorganized pit stops. Ultimately, Demler unsuccessfully attempted the shafting of Amick, Rocky, and even Rocky's haphazard crew by temporarily keeping all the prize money for himself.

For 1959, Rocky was in a volatile chief mechanic's partnership with Herb Porter on another laydown, a passionate pink Lesovsky. It sat on the pole but finished a galling third in the 500 with a malfunctioning rear suspension. Then with only 10 laps to go in 1960,

the same fast but annoying laydown was rapidly overtaking the 500's winning, warring Ken-Paul and Leader Card 1 Watsons until provoking further misery by blowing its engine. Rocky and Herb continued their uneasy union through 1962—far longer than anybody at the White Front predicted—and then emerged from it as racing foes vowing never to speak to one another for the rest of their roadster careers.

And so, having already spent time consorting with the likes of Pankratz, Demler, and Porter, it was only fair that Rocky in 1963 should make the acquaintances of interesting folks like Bruce Homeyer, Roger McCluskey, and Carl Nosal.

Knowing beforehand of Homeyer's dubious reputation as a car owner, and McCluskey's as an error-prone chauffeur, Rocky decided

Jud Phillips' drop-dead pretty "Too Much California" Konstant Hot sprint car. In only five tournaments it won three national titles, made obsolete every "Hoosier Clem" sprinter, and kept Roger McCluskey, Rocky Philipp, and Carl Nosal in groceries. *Scalzo collection*

that if he was going to earn any living at all as chief mechanic it was not going to be with Konstant Hot's new Watson, but with its phenomenal sprint car. Hauling the Konstant Hot out to L.A. over the winter, Rocky painstakingly preened and updated it at his garage on Crenshaw in North Hollywood. It was a fortunate thing. Without the prize money of the Konstant Hot sprinter, Rocky and Roger and Carl would have had almost no 1963 prize money at all.

Yet had the 1963 500 gone just a bit differently, the Konstant Hot trio would have had it made. Rocky had never previously worked on a Watson, but had a vast memory of the specifications of Offenhausers and dinosaurs generally. Unfortunately, Roger McCluskey had only gotten in a few miles of practice when he encountered a spinning funny car nose-to-nose, trashing the funny car and ripping off the Konstant Hot's own nose. After Rocky put on a fresh nose and the Konstant Hot had visited the Official Safety Station and gotten the magnaflux treatment, everything looked ace to Rocky all over again, even when Roger time-trialed only 14th quick. McCluskey, as Rocky well knew, was always a horrible qualifier anyway; besides, once the 500 started Roger figured to be so stimulated by the 13 dinosaurs and funny cars ahead of him that he'd be tearing after them as though they were rabbits. Accordingly, Rocky's prerace instructions to his driver were simple and basic: Avoid trouble on the 500's crowded, pushy, first lap; be occupying a steady position by the fifth lap; and from then until seeing the checkered flag be moving steadily forward and never surrender a position.

All the instructions went unheeded, just as Rocky had known in advance that they would be. McCluskey could never control or pace himself. He made four passes with the Konstant Hot in two laps, bulled into the top 10 at five, then became one of an 11-car pack trapped behind a roadblock of a Novi. After he blew off the Novi, he caught up to the 500's fastest lowbelly laydown. He blew it off too.

By now it was quite clear to Rocky and Carl that Roger had come to race, that he was driving the best 500 of his career, and that the Konstant Hot was very much a potential winner. In fact, after the leading Agajanian Willard Battery made a tire and refueling stop, Roger and the Konstant Hot actually went into first for 10 rousing miles. But still to come was Roger's own pit stop—which turned into a disaster. Unlike any other dinosaur team that 500 or ever, Rocky had equipped the Konstant Hot's tire-changing gang with pneumatic guns instead of wheel hammers. But McCluskey had his head in the wrong place as ever and when he bombed into his pit he overshot it and ended up in the wrong stall; Rocky had to

rap him on the helmet with his fist to make Roger move off the tire hose that his wheels had stopped on top of.

Underway again, Roger regained much of the racetrack that his pit stop had lost. As the 500 progressed he began mixing it up with two other Watsons, the Bryant Heating & Cooling 9 and the John Zink 52. They both crashed, and as the 500 wound down, he was up to third place, wiping his goggles with one hand while furiously gesturing with the other that the Agajanian Willard Battery just ahead of him was throwing off oil. Out on the third turn with five laps to go, Roger threw a wild, last gasp, attempted pass at the Willard Battery of the kind that only he seemed capable; and the resulting long slide and spin out which followed torpedoed the Konstant Hot from 3rd to 15th.

For once, Roger wasn't laughing. He was still so pissed when he got back to Gasoline Alley and the Konstant Hot garage that he up and kicked Rocky's beer refrigerator so hard that it carried a big dent for the rest of its existence.

The Agajanian Willard Battery's purported oil-spraying had made other dinosaur personalities hot as well, especially Eddie Sachs and his chief, Wally Meskowski. Sachs got so talkative about it that he ended up having Parnelli Jones deck him the next day at a victory luncheon. McCluskey hadn't attended the luncheon, nor had Rocky, and the peace-loving Rocky afterward decided it had been a damn good thing. The two of them might also have gotten decked.

Not too long afterward, Bruce Homeyer arbitrarily folded up his dinosaur operation, but permitted Rocky and Roger and Carl to go on campaigning the Konstant Hot sprint car. The three men ended up winning the national tournament, laughing all the way. They captured so many races and won so much prize money they had the other sprinter teams begging for mercy. Occasionally Rocky and Carl would share the booty by bringing biscuits and ground round to the White Front. Then they'd fry it up on the White Front stove for the other winless, starving teams to gratefully scarf down.

McCluskey's painful 1963 slip from 3rd to 15th with 5 miles to go was achieved at a cost in prize money of almost $50,000. Afterward, Rocky had accepted the drop in fortunes the philosophical way that dinosaur chiefs invariably did. First he'd telephoned his wife back in L.A. and told her, "Honey, you know that new swimming pool you wanted? Sorry, but it's down in the number three corner." And then he and Carl departed Gasoline Alley to take a rest and pass the remainder of the afternoon, night, and maybe even dawn getting their heads straight back at the White Front.

Roadster pit crews got the pleasure of living for their work. Not living in the financial sense, but in the enormous rush of satisfaction that went with watching and hearing their dinosaur roaring by and knowing there was a lot of each of them in it. This is the Bill Forbes team of chief Dave Laycock, his assistant Junior Dryer, as well as a collection of burly studs in cowboy boots who spoke in Texas accents because Laycock's roadster chauffeurs tended to come from there. *Indy 500 Photos*

LIKE THE TEARING OF BED SHEETS

It's one of the most exciting pieces of prose from roadster Indianapolis—Russ Catlin's account of 33 tall block Meyer-Drake Offenhausers opening up to full revs on the green flag lap of the 1955 500:

"Closing our eyes we waited for the indescribable sound we've heard for so many years. A frightening sound not unlike a thousand freight trains rushing through a tunnel and ending with a crescendo like the tearing of a thousand bed sheets. It was the full field pouring it on down the backstraight and then, with one last jab at the throttle, a shut off for the number 3 turn. Then the muted half murmur as the leaders hit the short straight. And then they came . . . zoom . . . zoom . . . zoom!"

Quite a few of the chief mechanics of the previous chapter who today have somewhat diminished hearing as a consequence of sharing all those Memorial Days together listening to their own and the other Meyer-Drakes are in serious disagreement with Catlin's description. He surely was one of the great racing writers, but Catlin had a tin ear for the Offy. Offys sounding like tearing bed sheets? No, the deep rumble and torque of their four cylinders taking hold was so heavy and dense that it seemed to shake the Speedway. And that "last jab of the throttle" business of Catlin's just never happened. If a roadster driver was doing his job, he never had the luxury of "jabbing" but was flat on his roadster's pedal to the bitter end.

Last, Catlin seems to have missed the biggest thing of all about the Offenhauser: the dramatic BOOM! reverberating out the chrome exhaust pipe as its driver at last came briefly off the throttle and disappeared balls out around Indy's 1 and 3 corners. It wasn't true, but so powerful was the old engine's myth that, to hear some people tell it, when you were racing an Offy around Indianapolis you required no brakes: The violent back pressure provided by the Meyer-Drake's 15-to-1 compression was all the stopping power necessary.

Listening to a Meyer-Drake Offenhauser roaring away in a Watson roadster was extra special. It was a dinosaur sound like nothing else. Because of engine placement, Epperly and Lesovsky lowbelly laydowns often had their exhausts pointing downward tom-tomming the track surface. But a Watson's shiny chrome steel exhaust, some 3 inches in diameter, came out of the left side of the engine bay, then extended back over the driver's shoulder past the Halibrand flip-top fuel cap to trumpet its message into the open Hoosier air. From headers to pipe tip, a Watson exhaust was 9 feet long. That gave the sound plenty of space to swell and echo.

And it gave bystanders and onlookers lots of grief. Red hot—as they always were at the conclusion of 500 racing miles—those 9 feet of chromed Watson exhaust spared nobody. In 1956, with Indy's Victory Circle typically overrun with VIPs and trophy queens, the exhaust pipe of the John Zink 8 took an especially wicked toll. Its victims included rubber honcho Raymond Firestone, who somewhat managed to fry his crotch against it—in some photographs Firestone is shown grimacing—and actress Virginia Mayo, who got one of her wrists pinked. And after the winning Leader Card 5 of 1959 succeeded in scorching the

As Indy's packed pit area and petrified mechanics watched in panic, the Bill Forbes Watson, and the Econo Car, an Epperly laydown, both entered pit road too hot in 1963 and had to take evasive action to miss one another; while pit crews of other teams scrambled for their lives, both dinosaurs twirled around and around without hitting anything. And not long afterward the Bill Forbes tried re-entering the pits, went into another long spin, and the same pit crews scrambled for their lives a second time. Its engine dead, a hole gouged in its tail where it had banged the inside wall, the Bill Forbes was pushed back to its stall and re-fired, whereupon it returned to the 500 and finished sixth. *Bob Tronolone*

A roadster's Meyer-Drake transmission was a glorified Model A Ford. Prone to overheating, it might cause all sorts of grief by locking in gear during pit stops. And chiefs and their crews listened in horror whenever their driver slipped and abused and fried the fragile clutch.

But even when a pit stop went well, getting a lumbering, hyperventilating roadster and its tall gear ratio underway again was a backbreaker, requiring the pushing of several straining mechanics. *Indy 500 Photo*

Taking split seconds to pump dozens of gallons of nitro-spiked methanol into his red-hot roadster during a crisis pit stop was dangerous duty for a chief mechanic. Johnnie Pouelsen demonstrates his derring-do. *Indy 500 Photos*

bare legs of starlet Erin O'Brien while she was in the process of bussing winning driver Rodger Ward, Hollywood reportedly issued a policy keeping its lovelies out of Victory Circle whenever a Watson roadster was there.

Furthermore, a thirsty Meyer-Drake drank so much methanol, wood alcohol, during a 500 that a typical Watson's Wayne Ewing fuel tank had to be refilled three times with a high-pressure fuel nozzle held directly above the 108 inches of molten exhaust pipe chrome. Considerable pain and grief resulted from this. In 1958, its exhaust pipe kinked and twisted from a collision, the John Zink 16 couldn't get any methanol unless its refueler almost rested his forearm against the bent pipe; the refueler, A. J. Watson, the Head himself, ended up heat-blistered and swaddled in bandages. And 1961 photographs of the Agajanian Willard Battery show that Johnnie Pouelsen semideflected the pipe problem by shortening and crimping the Watson exhaust so that it didn't extend over the fuel cap. But the crimped pipe ended up blasting raging exhaust fumes straight into Johnnie's face, so in later 500s he restored the original pipe. For his part, Watson was always prepared to sacrifice safety for

acoustics; he just didn't think that an Offy with a crimped pipe sounded like an Offy.

Many chief mechanics slipped a protective tube made out of stove pipe asbestos over their blazing hot exhausts during Indy refueling stops. And middle-aged volunteer members of the Speedway Safety Patrol wearing highly flammable street clothing stood by hopefully pointing the barrels of modest Co-2 extinguishers in the direction of every refueling. Nobody ever troubled to ask for any, but better safety conditions would have been a blessing. After all, to make refueling stops go faster, chiefs pumped volatile methanol into dinosaurs at ungodly high pressures, and holding onto a fueling line was almost like holding onto a fire hose. You had to be physically strong to lift up a big aircraft-type refueling hose full of methanol, and stronger still when you cracked open its nozzle and the pressure went crazy. Not surprisingly, being refueling man was a responsibility nobody on a five-man dinosaur pit crew much wanted, and with the exception of George Bignotti, who never liked that fire-hose feel, almost every roadster chief performed his own refueling. "It's the worst job, and on race day you don't want to bring in some new guy on the crew to have him burn you down," Jud Phillips once explained. Many a roadster didn't survive its refueling. Ramming a war surplus aircraft nozzle into a roadster's 5 1/2-inch fuel tank neck and then squeezing it open was itself tricky, because it was a double hole, fuel going in one side and up the other, and too much pressure caused it to swirl and foam. Yet a chief was willing to chance it in order to chaotically pump anywhere from 40 to 60 gallons in 20 seconds—holding his breath the whole time to keep from inhaling toxic fumes.

What every chief and his crew members worried about among themselves was a truly big fire breaking out one day. Not an ordinary fire, but roaring, rolling waves of pure heat and flame that nobody could see because methanol burns invisibly.

The right or wrong conditions never materialized, Indy never suffered The Big One, but in 1964 the Dayton Steel Wheel boys succeeded in setting their Watson ablaze. Buster Warke was the Dayton chief. A crewman jerked the asbestos free of the tailpipe before Buster had the refueling nozzle out. Fuel hit the pipe, and a flash fire took off inside the tank. Knowing what to do because he was fire-experienced, Buster slammed shut the Halibrand cap and smothered the flames—methanol carries no oxygen of its own. Dayton Steel Wheel's driver that year was Troy Ruttman, also well-versed in

In 1963, the Bryant Heating & Cooling 9, here getting serviced, spun out and stalled. That should have been the end of it, because roadsters weren't equipped with self-starters,once you spun one of the mothers out, you had to suffer the consequence of feeling foolish sitting there with the grandstands staring at you. However, a crew of emergency workers in a push truck succeeded in getting the Bryant going again. Driver Eddie Sachs continued on for another haulin' ten minutes, threw a wheel, and hit almost head-on into the wall. Damage all repaired, Eddie and the Bryant were racing hard all over again just two months later at the Milwaukee 200. *Indy 500 Photos*

refueling emergencies because in prior 500s other refuelers had lit him up twice. So while fire swirled around the Dayton Steel Wheel, big Troy executed the basic roadster driver drill of hanging tough and staying in the saddle until the flames got put out. Then he rejoined the 500.

That 1964 500 was very close to the end of the roadster age, and the four-overhead-camshaft, V-8, Ford-powered Lotuses with their bag-of-snakes exhaust headers and strange scream very much had the roadsters and their antique Offenhausers on the run. In a belated gesture of support, Indianapolis and the United States Auto Club permitted roadster teams to do desperate things, including hauling greater fuel loads than they ever had previously. To defeat the funny cars, Johnnie Pouelsen believed that he, Parnelli Jones, and J. C. Agajanian would have to make fewer pit stops. So Johnnie went to the extreme of fitting the Agajanian Bowes Seal Fast with a monster tank whose methanol capacity was 90 gallons. And to save some pounds,

Chickie Hirashima, a sorcerer of the Meyer-Drake, made himself A. J. Watson's Offy guru. Hardly anybody could equal him at making a monolith Offy stand up and wail for 500 miles, and Chickie was the mill man socking horsepower into the Leader Card 5, the Ken-Paul, and the Leader Card 3, all Indy winners. *Indy 500 Photos*

he had Eddie Kuzma make it out of thin-gauge aluminum rather than boilerplate steel.

Well, the Agajanian Bowes Seal Fast with its big and deadly fuel tank managed to be in and out of the lead and was doing pretty well until its fateful first and last pit stop, when almost the same scenario as the Dayton Steel Wheel repeated itself. Somebody on the Agajanian crew boo-booed and apparently pulled away the asbestos shield too hastily. Methanol dripped onto the tailpipe, and fire spread to the tank. This fire was far worse than the Dayton Steel Wheel's, however, because Johnnie Pouelsen had had the Agajanian Bowes Seal Fast chug-a-lugging a cocktail of methanol spiked with nitromethane, and nitro does contain its own oxygen. So slamming shut the fuel cap couldn't smother the invisible fire inside; instead, just as Parnelli Jones had the Agajanian Bowes Seal Fast on its way back down the pit road, all the trapped heat and chemical fumes ignited—KABLOOEY!—and the giant but fragile tank exploded into several pieces.

At first Parnelli didn't realize that he had a fireball raging behind him, but he noticed the cockpit of the Agajanian Bowes Seal Fast filling up with raw fuel, then saw all the other teams frantically waving him down, and suddenly felt excruciating heat. For once saying to hell with the driver code of going down with a flaming roadster, Parnelli saved his life by unbuckling the belts and bailing out to leave the Agajanian Bowes Seal Fast burning itself out on the wide-open spaces of the pit road. He probably saved other lives in the pit area too, as the Agajanian Bowes Seal Fast's fire was enormous, a horrible conflagration, and might well have spread to all the other pit stalls and fuel storage tanks.

A gorging Offenhauser devoured a gallon of methanol every 3 1/2 miles and chewed up a set of Firestones at that same pitch. By the time its Offy was ready to run dry of fuel, a roadster's rubber was almost threadbare as well.

Working just as hard as a roadster's refuelers, then, was its four-man gang of tire changers. Halibrand kidney-bean wheels made of alloy or magnesium were locked onto the axles by big, three-eared, Halibrand knock-off nuts. And with the exception of Rocky Philipp's 1963 Konstant Hot quartet operating with power wrenches, wheel changers removed them with smashes from copper or lead hammers with wooden handles. Often one good blow was sufficient for a tire changer to bang a knock-off free and spin it loose, then rip away the wheel and worn Firestone and run up a fresh one walloped snug with two more hammer blows—being extra-careful not to mistakenly wham the valve stem and flatten the tire. Truly deft changers were already crouching down banging away on the knock-offs long before a roadster got cranked up in the air by a hand jack. And to shave approximately six more seconds off tire changes, around 1959 crews started using compressed oxygen to raise roadsters off the ground by means of four steel legs descending from the chassis.

If the tire changers were really coordinated, they finished up their labors just as the refuelers completed theirs, and just as the guy using the 6-foot-long pole to pass the driver a clean set of goggles had completed his. Then, while the driver was simultaneously pampering the notorious Meyer-Drake transmission (a glorified Model A Ford that seemed to enjoy locking up and refusing to go back into gear), as well as praying he wasn't going to overheat and fry the equally suspect clutch, and while all four cylinders worth of Offenhauser were barking and shaking and protesting, the whole pit crew joined in the backbreaking ballet of pushing away the lumbering, hyperventilating, overweight roadster with its tall gear ratio. A dinosaur and its Offy circled Indy in one gear, and there was a second, lower gear for pulling out of the pits. Strangely, there was also a third gear—reverse. This gear was a holdover from the Speedway's passenger car–based "junkyard formula" of the thirties, but nobody had any idea what it meant in the fifties and sixties because they no longer raced stocks.

Drivers left the Offenhauser running during pit stops. Everybody worried that if they ever shut one down, maybe they'd never get the ornery devil lit off again. Shaking to life an Offy's 345 pounds of hardened steel, brass, bronze, and aluminum was quite a physical act. First a drone aircraft inertia starter got jammed into the roadster's nose. This was a big broomstick-like gizmo, and yet another piece of war surplus. Whoever was operating it knew that if the shaft ever kicked back it could fracture his arm. And then, slowly and reluctantly, the rods and pistons and crank began rotating, until finally the whole works were vibrating and roaring.

"They were good old warhorses," fondly remarked one chief mechanic. For all its vibrating and shaking, the Offy was just as easy to work on and maintain as a dinosaur roadster was; the two made a terrific match. And because the essential Meyer-Drake Offenhauser was a hoary four decades old, it made a wonderfully handsome-looking monolith with its great barrel crankcase and other classic features. Long-in-the-tooth or not, at Indianapolis or anywhere else in championship racing, there wasn't another engine you could purchase that would keep up with the Offy, or match one's longevity.

"Bulletproof," somebody described the Offy, and decades of Offenhauser development and inbreeding truly made one seem that way. Meyer-Drake's asking price for an Offy was roughly $10,000 per engine, however, a lot of money in a racing era not of modern profligacy. And so, when Bob Wilke of Leader Card had once instructed A. J. Watson to "always buy the best," Watson understood that Wilke hadn't meant it literally. About the best any roadster chief could expect from a car owner was a brand new Offenhauser every month of May, along with the understanding that the chief keep it alive and potent not only for an Indy's 500 miles but the three or four 100- and 200-mile championships at Milwaukee and Trenton. All chiefs had been brought up in the tradition of economy, learning to be frugal and make used parts last. They knew how to patch together an Offy like an old set of trousers when necessary.

Not even a name change could rescue the fortunes of Parnelli Jones and his hoodooed Agajanian Willard Battery. Freshly christened the Agajanian Bowes Seal Fast for its swan song 500 of 1964, it succeeded in exploding and burning out on pit road. Parnelli: "Leaving the pits, I threw out a cup of water, and everything went POOF! I thought it was water hitting the exhaust pipe. Actually, the whole back of the fuel tank had blown off and I was already burning without knowing it. Some of the other pit crews could see the heat waves and started waving their arms. So I backed off the throttle. And when I did I looked down and saw about 4 inches of unburned fuel down in the belly pan. You've seen these pictures of people in fires jumping out of skyscraper windows instead of getting burned? I was only going about 30 miles per hour, but it wouldn't have mattered if I'd been doing 170. When that fuel took off and started the cockpit on fire I unbuckled and jumped the hell out of there." *Bob Tronolone, Indy 500 Photos*

The STP Novi, a Kurtis-Kraft powered by one of the notorious and supercharged V-8 Novis, was out practicing in 1959 when the crankshaft ripped free of its moorings and there was a cataclysmic unloading. Spewing debris and flaming engine oil, the lashing, pirouetting beast bounced off three different walls and never stopped until its ever-flailing crankshaft blew out the bottom of the cylinder block and gouged a furrow in the race track of 1,941 feet, six-and-a-half football fields. *Bob Tronolone*

blew the face off the Meyer-Drake block, came close to mangling the drag link steering, and then the Kelso spun out, burning in its own oil slick.

"Ring," "timing gear," "piston," "fuel pump," "crankshaft," and "fuel injection," are failures that the *Indianapolis News 500-Mile Race Record Book* credits with crippling Offenhausers in one 500 or another. And there was yet another small but vital component with a history of killing the Offy. When it came time to wire their dinosaurs for electricity, chief mechanics continued their dependence on the war surplus market by using, mostly, Joe Hunt Magnetos, which were hopped-up versions of Bendix-Scintilla aviation magnetos. Originally intended to spark small and low-revving airplane engines, at Indy they had to do it at the speed of an Offy's crankshaft—roughly 6,000 throbbing, revving revolutions per minute. It was more than twice the velocity they'd been designed for. It amounted to a boggling 2.9 million high-voltage sparks cranked out every minute, so it was no wonder that its mag was the Offy's most overstressed accessory.

No new Kuzma, Epperly, Lesovsky, Kurtis-Kraft, or Watson came complete with a Meyer-Drake Offenhauser, but virtually everybody purchasing a roadster put an Offy in it, because outside of a Novi that was almost the only engine that fit in the bay.

The co-builders Dale Drake and Louie Meyer were said to be of differing opinions about their Offenhauser. Drake welcomed experiments and changes. Meyer, on the other hand, preferred keeping development expenses to a minimum, wanting everything that came out of Meyer-Drake to be equal. Let the individual chief mechanics perform their own soup-ups.

And many of the chiefs did. But just as it was with all dinosaur speed secrets, it was difficult for one chief to get an advantage over another because all knowledge was routinely shared. If you were a

An Offy was constructed to surmount adversity, and as a vote for the apparent indestructibility of Meyer-Drake crankshafts, wrist pins, camshafts, cylinder blocks, and bearing webs, certain chiefs, during a 500, spared their drivers the extra responsibility of having to study dashboard instruments like oil and water pressure by blanking them out with masking tape. But "bulletproof" was a term that didn't strictly apply. Just like roadsters themselves, Offys did break down, particularly if one was allowed to wear out and vibrate itself to pieces. Then it could become spectacular. In 1961, the Kelso Auto Dynamics, a matte black Lesovsky laydown with an out-of-whack chassis, was belting around the Brickyard for test lap after test lap, its driver white-knuckled and wringing wet and its tall tires singing in "the voice of Firestone." Finally, after 900 hard but useless reconnaissance miles, the Offy came unglued. A flailing connecting rod

continued on page 101

Color Gallery

Above: In 1957 and 1958, Epperly Offy laydowns like the Belond Special 9 controlled Indy, capturing two 500s; but the sidewinder design didn't stick. From 1959 through 1964, the force was back with the upright Offy dinosaurs, Indy champions six consecutive times. *Bob Tronolone*

Left: Elements of the John Zink team pushing their No. 52 Watson to its starting position on the outside of the front row of the 1957 Indy 500 might as well not have bothered. Troy Ruttman put No. 52 into the lead, then had it overheat and expire in only 13 laps. *Bob Tronolone*

Right: Jack Turner, driver of the Bardahl 45 Kurtis-Kraft, had a thorny career. In 1961, No. 45 roughed him up by going violently upside down near the start-finish strip. In 1962, Jack tipped over again, this time in turn 4, breaking a toe plus his pelvis. In 1963, when he was out doing warm-ups, he turned turtle a third straight time, doing a number on his vertebrae. "Cactus" Jack used the episode as an excuse to hang it up. *Bob Tronolone*

Below: The original Watson roadster, the 1956 Indy-winning John Zink 8, became the John Zink 25 in 1957. Its narrow cockpit enlarged to accommodate big Jud Larson, it missed qualifying for the 500, but later that summer at the Hoosier Hundred got its initiation on a dirt track. Then in 1958, as the John Zink 44, Jud again driving, it successfully qualified and finished the 500 eighth. Over the same winter, it was scaled down to the dimensions of a John Zink champ dirt car. Later still it became an economy super-modified and was raced to oblivion on Oklahoma short tracks. *Bob Tronolone*

Above left. The Dart-Kart 83, a copycat Watson constructed by Floyd Trevis and raced by rookie Donnie Davis, created consternation in the 1961 500. Engine oil from a ruptured tank seeped on the tires, precipitating a long spin and slide across the front straightaway. Abandoning No. 83 as soon as the spinning stopped, Donnie chose to walk across the track into the pits. Four other drivers—including Cactus Jack Turner—cracked up their roadsters, barely missing him. *Bob Tronolone*

Above right: Jim Rathmann, chief mechanic Smokey Yunick, and the Simoniz 4 Watson. Coming off the fourth row, Rathmann led early, then had to quit the 1961 500 with a sparkless magneto. *Bob Tronolone*

Left: Gasoline Alley, 1961. *Bob Tronolone*

Above: Left to right, Jim Hurtubise, Parnelli Jones, and Shorty Templeman. *Bob Tronolone*

Opposite: A. J. Foyt, Eddie Sachs, and Rodger Ward, the one, two, and three finishers of the 1961 500. Foyt, leading, made an emergency fuel stop and Sachs inherited a 25-second lead just as he glanced over and saw his right rear tire going to cord with 16 laps to go. With three laps to go, Sachs decided to stop for rubber, and Foyt took him. Ward might have defeated the pair of them had he not run a cautious 500 because a race-long rattle in the underbelly had him imagining that a U-joint to the driveshaft was preparing to fracture. *Bob Tronolone*

Above: Pole position car and third-place finisher in 1959, and fifth with a blown engine in 1960, Lujie Lesovsky's Racing Associates 10, Paul Goldsmith up, fell out of the 1961 500 with an oil leak. In 1962, Donnie Davis brought it in fourth. *Bob Tronolone*

Right: Lujie Lesovsky. *Bob Tronolone*

Opposite: George Bignotti pushing his dinosaur. *Bob Tronolone*

Inset: A. J. Foyt and Bowes Seal Fast crew, 1962. *Bob Tronolone*

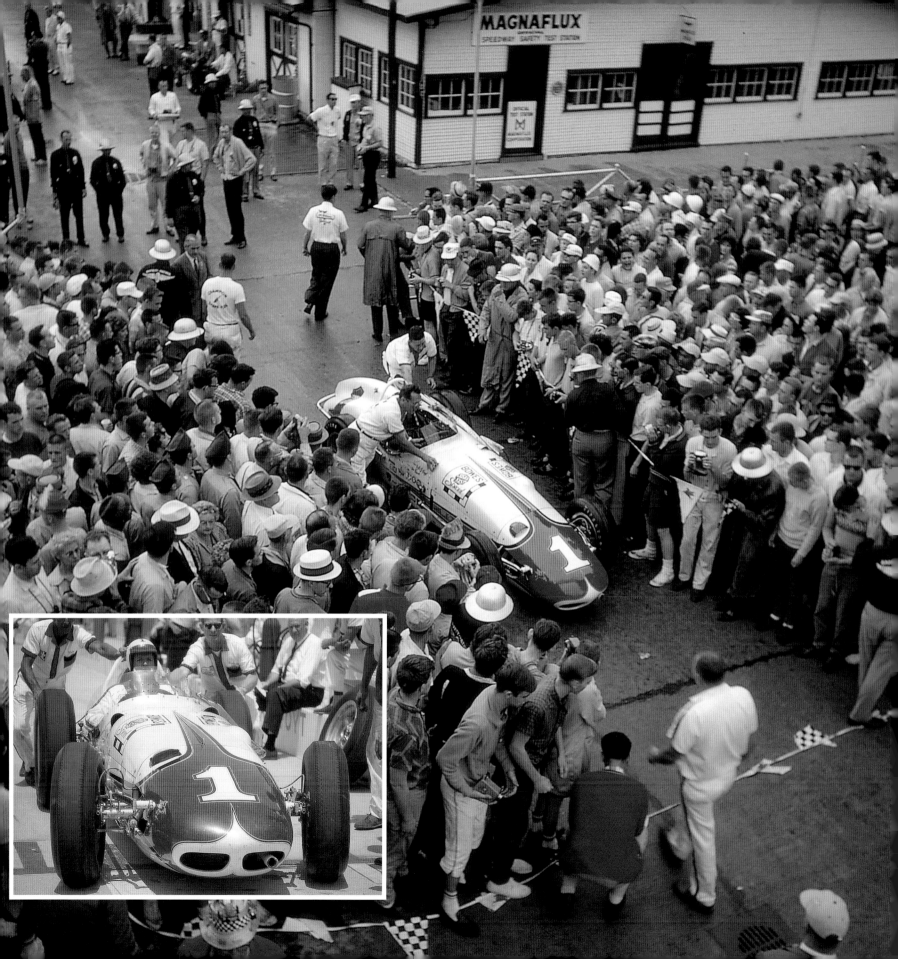

Rookie Jimmy McElreath did stirring things in the 1962 500 with the Schultz Fuel Equipment 15, a Kurtis-Kraft/Watson crossbreed. *Bob Tronolone*

Pace lap, 1962. Getting ready to get it on. *Bob Tronolone*

Above: Parnelli Jones, J. C. Agajanian, and "Calhoun" broke the one-minute Brickyard lap. *Bob Tronolone*

Left: Big, big Memorial Day for team Leader Card in 1962: a one, two 500 finish for Rodger Ward and Len Sutton. *Bob Tronolone*

Top left: Their third 500 together in 1963 was finally the charm for the Agajanian Willard Battery 98 and Parnelli Jones, Indy winners at 143.137 miles per hour. *Bob Tronolone*

Top right: Don Branson's Leader Card 4 of 1963 was the 13th Watson to come off of A. J.'s dinosaur assembly line at 421 West Palmer, Glendale. New in 1962, when it was the Leader Card 3, Rodger Ward used it to win Indy and two other national title meets. Branson and No. 4 finished fifth in the 1963 500; two years later, in 1965, at Phoenix International Raceway, they won the last match a dinosaur team ever won. *Bob Tronolone*

Above: The Demler 99 had a long and full history. Originally constructed in 1961 as the Leader Card 41, it was one of two unsuccessful coil-over Watsons. In 1962, rebuilt and refitted with torsion bars and named the Leader Card 7, the automobile was an Indy runner-up, but later got badly wrecked at Milwaukee. Repaired and rebuilt all over again, it was sold and renamed the Demler 99. In 1963 it ran Indy's fifth fastest time trial at 150.163 miles per hour. And in the 1964 500, here, it finished fourth and made its ill-fated driver Johnny White Rookie-of-the-Year. *Bob Tronolone*

Top: Only one of these three Watsons from the 1964 500 fared well. The Bill Forbes 18, piloted by Lloyd Ruby, came in third. The Chapman 23, Dick Rathmann up, could only take seventh, three laps down. And Jim Hurtubise in the Tombstone Life 56 went out at 430 miles with an oil leak. *Bob Tronolone*

Above left: Larry Pfitzenmaier, a retired 30-year Navy captain and jet fighter pilot who in the Vietnam War dropped an A-4 Skyhawk onto short carrier runways in the middle of the Pacific about 250 times on as many combat missions, owns and drives the Simoniz 16 of 1959. It's the only Watson roadster that gets raced regularly in vintage events. *Larry Pfitzenmaier*

Above right: In August 1995, the Simoniz 16 got towed 6,704 round-trip miles from Larry's home in La Plata, Maryland, to California and the annual race car beauty contest on the sprawling golf links at elegant Pebble Beach. It captured the Tony Hulman Cup and also swept the postwar, open-cockpit race car category. *Larry Pfitzenmaier*

Kurtis-Krafts were among the biggest dinosaurs. This is one of the hexed V-8 Novis, recipient of a blown transmission on the 1965 500's opening lap. *Bob Tronolone*

Champion of the 1961 500 with a new speed record, the Bowes Seal Fast, a Watson-Trevis, was one of the wonder roadsters. During 1962 and 1963 it scored three additional victories at Milwaukee and Trenton. *Bob Tronolone*

Among the oddest roadster combinations was the Racing Associates 22. Somehow it managed to mate the coachwork of a Watson upright to the chassis of a Dennie Moore lowbelly laydown. Part of a three-dinosaur Herb Porter team, it fell victim to the front straightaway's giant wreck of 1961. Today this oddball resides in a museum in the Netherlands. *Bob Tronolone*

Sometimes you needed a score card to keep up with name and number changes. The Coral Harbour 15 Watson of 1961, here, was in 1959 the Simoniz 16, in 1960 the Dowgard 2, and in 1962 and 1963 the Drewry's 88. *Bob Tronolone*

Below: After racking up consecutive wins with his Belond Equa-Flow laydown in 1957 and 1958, builder and chief mechanic George Salih had less success with his Metal-Cal Special of 1960. In three 500s, it finished 19th, 6th, and 10th. *Bob Tronolone*

Haulin' the mail into turn 4, a Watson chases a Kurtis-Kraft. *Bob Tronolone*

Right: Designed for Smokey Elisian, but raced by Eddie Sachs, the Dean Van Lines sat on two Indy pole positions, then racked up runner-up and third place finishes in the dramatic 500s of 1961 and 1962. One of many replica Watsons, its constructor was the wondrous flake, Fat Boy Ewing. *Bob Tronolone*

Back with a new name in 1962 after blowing its motor in five miles the previous year, the Bryant Heating & Cooling 54, another fast but luckless Epperly lay-down, unofficially exceeded 150 miles per hour while practicing, started the 500 on the front row, then stumbled to a fifth place finish. *Bob Tronolone*

Elmer George, son-in-law of Indy Motor Speedway President Tony Hulman, was a sprint car champion and erratic roadster driver in the 500. In 1957 he cracked up trying to get lined-up for the start, and in 1962, despite relief help from Paul Russo and A. J. Foyt, Elmer's Sarkes-Tarzian—a Lujie Lesovsky copy of a Watson—had a pit fire and finished 17th. *Bob Tronolone*

Diehard roadster soldier Lloyd Ruby raced different dinosaurs in five consecutive 500s. In 1960 he won rookie of the year honors with the Agajanian 98; in 1961 finished 8th in the Autolite 5; in 1962, here, finished 8th in the Thompson Industries 12; in 1963 finished 19th after crashing the John Zink 52; and in 1964 Ruby had his best finish, 3rd, in the Bill Forbes 18. *Bob Tronolone*

Opposite: Eddie Sachs and the Dean Van Lines 2, here tailing Johnny Boyd in the Metal-Cal 38, was on a flier in the 1962 500: from 27th starting hole to 3rd place by the finish. *Bob Tronolone*

Inset: The Autolite 5, variously known as the Detroiter Mobile Homes and the Mid-Continental Securities 14, was another heart-breaking Epperly. *Bob Tronolone*

Outlasting the brittle funny cars in 1964, the Sheraton-Thompson 1 Watson and A. J. Foyt took the 500 and set a roadster track record of 147.350 miles per hour. *Bob Tronolone*

A. J. Watson's last season for cracking out Indy roadsters was 1963, and he made five including the Bardahl 45, victim of a blown engine at 275 miles. *Bob Tronolone*

Right: Moving in on Jim Hurtubise in the Tombstone Life 56, Lloyd Ruby in the Bill Forbes 18 races on to his 1964 career-best Brickyard finish of third. *Bob Tronolone*

Righteously battling funny cars all day long in the 1965 500, Gordon Johncock outlasted most of them, wrestling the Weinberger Homes 76 Watson to an honorable fifth position This was the last great dinosaur drive. *Bob Tronolone*

Continued from page 81

chief wanting to know what grind of high-lift camshaft another chief was running, you just visited him at his garage in Gasoline Alley, or else traded information back and forth at the White Front.

After having painstakingly taught himself all its bumps and heavy vibrations, Chickie Hirashima had few equals at making an Offy stand up and wail for 500 miles. His big breakthrough occurred in 1957, when he shortened up the stroke and awoke the rods to serious revs. Builder of the winning Meyer-Drakes in at least three 500s, Chickie was more secretive, or maybe modest, than most. Exactly what black magic he laid on to make an Offy rip and roar

that way was something he never revealed. Instead, when in Chickie's estimation one of his big four-bangers had performed successfully, he would say, "Well, I guessed right." And when in his estimation one of them hadn't, he would say, "Well, I guessed wrong."

George Bignotti, who later became Louie Meyer's son-in-law, may have kept the most Offy secrets of anybody. He used special pistons, ran rich jets, and liked big Winfield camshafts. Occasionally he had custom machining performed on his cylinder blocks, and George had also been experimenting with super-strong titanium connecting rods until one of them got loose and flailed away cutting in half a whole block. Because standard No. 4 Meyer-Drake intake and exhaust camshafts were volatile and when buzzed

A Joe Hunt magneto was a Bendix-Scintilla unit that Hunt had completely redesigned, rebalanced, and souped up with goodies such as platinum points. It cost around $200. A 500 fanatic who was proud of his products, Hunt, whenever his mags were maligned, became resentful (Joe was among the most in-your-face personalities of the in-your-face dinosaur period). Yet maligned Joe Hunt magnetos frequently were; mag failure appeared to be the worst killer of the Offy. "Appeared" is the crucial qualifier, though, because many an irate chief mechanic who first jumped to the conclusion that the mag had gone belly up might later undertake an Offy autopsy and discover that the failure that actually put his roadster out of a 500 had been something else. *Bob Tronolone*

One of the best roadster 500s was in 1962. Several individual dinosaurs were having great runs. The Leader Card 3 and Leader Card 7, for instance, were finishing one-two; the Agajanian Willard Battery was rocketing along with the leaders despite no brakes; the Dean Van Lines was making a charge from 27th to 3rd; and, not least, the Bell Lines Trucking was roller-coastering close to the lead despite two traumatic pit stops. Roger McCluskey was on the pedal. On the first stop, the tranny refused to come out of gear until Roger gave the shift lever a fearsome whack with a wheel hammer. On the second stop the Bell overshot the pits and had to be dragged back to its stall. Hitting the bricks again, Roger was in scorching form all over again until the bracket holding a radiator overflow hose pinched the hose shut. Coolant collected in the belly pan beneath the engine. And just as the Bell and Roger were hauling around the north corner, spilled coolant struck the left rear Firestone and everything looped out. *Bob Tronolone*

too tightly could tear up everything in the Offy, Bignotti felt especially fortunate to have formed a special friendship with Ed Winfield. Winfield was a hop-up artist who was almost a scientist, and his eye for detail was so perfect that he ground not only camshafts but his own eye glasses, plus the lens of a telescope for scoping out the moon.

George won't confirm it, but throughout the dinosaur epoch he was said to be one of the strongest advocates for the horsepower benefits of nitromethane. Nitro was the same liquid and colorless "pop" that in 1964 helped set afire and blow apart the Agajanian Bowes Seal Fast. Subjected to 2,000 pounds of pressure and 500 degrees of heat, pop didn't merely burn, it detonated. Used in correct dosages, the stuff would wake up an Offy like nothing else; but if a chief mechanic got crazy with his pop, the result could be cataclysmic. Literally. Pistons, connecting rods, and crankshaft all could be eviscerated by pop going off inside an Offy, and the searing explosion that followed could disembowel a cylinder block and heave its shrapnel hundreds of feet

so that shredded Meyer-Drake hardware sometimes reached Indy grandstands.

Another powerful advocate of pop was Johnnie Pouelsen, and gung-ho Johnnie truly made many far-reaching contributions to the history of the Offenhauser, to the dinosaur roadster, and to the Indy career of Parnelli Jones. But Pouelsen once did something that was terrible. In 1964 he conjured up a bunch of "improvements" to try to drub a little more speed out of the doomed Agajanian Bowes Seal Fast. In addition to streamlining its cowl and oil tanks, adding science to its wheels with Bonneville-type plates, and repositioning the torsion bars and radiator, Johnnie committed aesthetic assault and battery by fitting the Agajanian's long and elegant Watson hood with a grotesquely ugly open-mouth air scoop.

Maybe it was a surprise that no rival chief had thought of doing so earlier. Even the dumb-dumbs knew that the more air an Offenhauser breathed, the more power it made. Every Offy, all the chiefs liked to say, was nothing but an "air pump," or a "heat pump." Ex-Air Force staff sergeant Herb Porter used to be so adamant about the latter term that he'd tyrannically line up all of his helpers at Racing Associates and, as if it were a drill, bark at them, "What is an Offy?" and give them no peace until they learned to repeat, "An Offy is a heat pump!" In 1953 and 1954 500s, Jim Travers and Frank Coons added ram-air velocity scoops to the Fuel Injection Special that gave Billy Vukovich a 30-horsepower edge over everybody else, and the Rich Kids had managed to keep their big air pump secret until Larry Shinoda, A. J. Watson's bird-dog and snoop, found out about it and took the information to Watson. The Head typically shared the news with everyone. And once it was out of the bag that an Offenhauser's Hilborn fuel injection breathed better on al fresco air than it did on a diet of the overheated and contaminated junk trapped under the hood, ram stacks came bursting out of all roadster engine bays. In identical fashion, once Johnnie Pouelsen's unscientific, but brutally efficient, open-mouth air scoop became known as "the poor man's supercharger" for its ability to suck so much additional air into the Offy, other roadsters started having their own classic hoods chopped up and defaced with big-mouth scoops. It was an aesthetic loss comparable to the crippling one wrought by wide, fat tires.

*S*omebody told me once that with the exception of Johnnie Pouelsen's Agajanian Willard Battery/Bowes Seal Fast and George Bignotti's Sheraton-Thompson 1, none of the other chief mechanics got much more than 400 horsepower out of their Offenhausers. But somebody else told me, no, the really stout Offys were those of Bruce Crower, Chickie Hirashima, and of course Herb Porter. Among chiefs, the prestige accorded to the guy who made the most horses was a huge ego deal. To Herb Porter, with the sometime-nickname of "Herbie Horsepower," it was almost the only deal. One of the most intense embarrassments of Herb's career, in fact, involved Offenhausers and horsepower. At the 1963 500, Herb's Racing Associates 46 had gotten bumped from the starting field, so Herb's patron and driver Ebb Rose had to rent a faster Watson roadster, the Sheraton-Thompson 32, to bump his way back into the show. And because the Sheraton-Thompson was powered by one of Bignotti's Offys, the humiliating message that went out afterward was that George built faster Offys than Herb.

But in 1966 Herb subsequently rebounded from this setback by producing the raging Godzilla of a dinosaur that was powered by what was hands-down the mightiest Offy of the era. It was the Racing Associates 39, a storming Watson that gulped in so much super-heated air it made Johnnie Pouelsen's open-mouth scoop look anemic by comparison. Ripping the Speedway's front and back straightaways at better than 200 miles per hour, and in the turns cracking off a giant thunderbolt of flame, the monster was credited with the fastest time trial ride a dinosaur ever made: 10 flailing miles averaging 158.367, or a full 3 miles per hour faster than the old Agajanian Bowes Seal Fast, the second fastest–ever dinosaur. And in addition to reaping such glory, Herb earned the everlasting distinction of being the last chief mechanic to make a roadster go fast enough to qualify to start in a 500.

How was he able to swing all this? By stepping up at the last moment and volunteering for the long-shot assignment of mating an Offenhauser to a turbocharger.

The Racing Associates 39—the ex-Racing Associates 46 of 1963, and the ex-Bardhal 86 of 1964—set its power and speed records when Indianapolis still followed an engine formula permitting a normally aspirated Offenhauser some 85 more cubic inches of displacement than a super- or turbocharged one, 256 to 170. Nobody disputed that a blower's muscle would easily overcome the handicap of those missing 85 inches in a sprint. The problem was making a blown dinosaur live for 500 miles. The Novis hadn't been able to, nor through the years had Herb. His wartime aviation days overhauling P-40s and P-51s had made him encyclopedic about compressors, inducers, and impellers that shrieked along at 40,000 revolutions. Accordingly, Herb was about the most outspoken proponent going of supercharging and turbocharging.

Beginning in the late forties and early fifties, he'd campaigned an Offy sprint car with a centrifugal open-face blower that briefly became the terror of Salem Speedway. And he'd had an even faster supercharged Indy champ dirt car that always went like stink through the first 50 miles, then burned out its bearings. It wasn't until years afterward, Herb once told me, he discovered that the "assholes" who'd supposedly been assisting him with the engineering had betrayed him by switching the impeller rate without ever telling him. And hadn't Herb gotten jobbed at the 1952 Indianapolis? His driver, Andy Linden, was moaning about the shrieking supercharger hurting his ears, so Herb addressed the problem by stuffing them with cotton and rendering Linden stone deaf; whereupon Andy went out to qualify and apparently put Herb's blown job on the pole position. But this was a 500 when the Speedway was bending its rules to accommodate the entry of a lumbering Cummings turbocharger diesel of 401 inches. And after this big illegal barge proceeded to lap faster, Herb got screwed out of the pole.

The seasons went by without Herb losing his faith in the potential of Offys with blowers, even though he stopped aggravating

---

Following pages: Named that because it looked like one, a "can of ham" oil tank was a teardrop of steel, sometimes sealed with fiberglass, held on by three spears of 4130 tubing. When full it contained about 15 quarts of 50 weight. Its history was odd. Photographs of Watson's first roadster, the John Zink 8, reveal that it was designed to carry its lubricant in a suitcase-shaped tank next to the driver's compartment; the Head, however, later changed his mind and decided to store the oil supply beneath the hood, on the right side above the axle. Later he changed his mind again and concluded that if he hung the 56 pounds near the left front that the wheel might stay better planted. Also there was the bonus of separating the oil from the engine heat. But for all the offense the various cans of ham gave, Watson might have been better off leaving everything under the hood. 500 miles of pounding and fierce Offenhauser vibration regularly subjected cans of ham to stress fractures causing them to crack open and slick the track. *Indy 500 Photos*

himself trying to develop them—until 1966 that is, when events suddenly made them appear viable at last.

Upheaval and turmoil were everywhere in 1966. Having just barely recovered from the shock of having the 500 wrested away from the dinosaurs and turned over to the funny cars, Indianapolis now was experiencing the spectacle of Goodyear warring with Firestone to terminate the long Flintstone domination. And on the engine front, Meyer-Drake Offenhauser was taking serious hits from Ford Motor Company, which had arranged the defection from the partnership of Louie Meyer so he could come to Ford and help develop and distribute its V-8 four-cam, the FoMoCo engine that in 1965 broke the long Offy dynasty by sweeping the 500's first four places. For Offenhauser, things had gone beyond desperate. Even A. J. Watson had defected to Ford. And during practice for that same 1965 500, there'd been the heresy of the Leader Card 95—making unsuccessful test laps with a howling four-cammer Ford wedged beneath the hood.

And while Offenhauser was in the midst of losing the engine war to Ford, Goodyear appeared to be losing the rubber one to Firestone, despite being the far larger corporation. So somebody from Goodyear had fatefully inquired, what might happen if on the quiet Goodyear started helping out those Indy teams on its rubber by coming to tiny Offenhauser's rescue with funds to invent a turbocharged version of the about-to-go-extinct Offy that would blow off all the Fords? And what if Goodyear used Herb Porter as R&D man?

The caper wasn't quite as straightforward as that, you understand—there were a few additional twists—but essentially that was the way it went down. And in the aftermath, all Herb's faith and pronouncements were vindicated: for good or ill, turbocharging took firm hold of the 500. A Goodyear-shod turbocharged Offy won the 1968 500, and for 27 of the following 28 Memorial Days throughout 1996, nothing but a turbocharged Offy, Ford, Cosworth, or Ilmore ever won a 500 or occupied a pole position, and some of those winning engines were Herb's.

Despite this, when in the course of my research it was necessary for me to go talk to Herb about the Racing Associates 39, I was somewhat reluctant. After all, the concept of turbocharging got pretty well discredited in 1996 when Indianapolis outlawed it. And the Racing Associates 39 roadster itself was not exactly an unqualified success. Although some people might still consider him "father of the turbocharger," Herb had always believed he never got all the notice he deserved. Some years before I'd heard him say as much, putting the blame on "the cocksuckers of the press." None of this boded well for a successful interview.

The interrogation began with me asking him if he still felt he'd not gotten sufficient credit for the Racing Associates 39 turbocharger project. It was my big mistake.

"*Credit?*" Herb demanded. "I'll tell you about *credit*. I'll tell you that little story. When I got that Goodyear engine going, at one of the first meetings I ever had with Goodyear management, our so-called racing press had already done some write-ups about it. And Goodyear wanted its part in the project to be top secret.

So some Goodyear vice president at the meeting got up waving around these write-ups asking, 'Since when did Goodyear get in the engine business?' And I answered, 'Hey, I can't help what these cocksuckers write!' Later I went back to the reporters and told them, 'Listen, you assholes, you gotta soft-pedal. You can't use my name or Goodyear's.' Which is why, later, a lot of other guys who didn't have a fuckin' thing to do with getting the turbocharger going ended up getting a fuckin' lot more ink than I ever did."

Herb motioned me to get my tape recorder rolling.

"Goodyear wanted a turbocharged Offy and I said I'd build one. This was April or so of 1966. The 500 was a month away, and I didn't have much Goodyear money, didn't have an engine, didn't even have a driver until my good friend Johnnie Pouelsen sent Bobby Grim over to my garage. 'Bobby,' I said, 'I've got some tests to do. Going to put a turbocharger in an old Watson roadster. Drive the sumbitch for me and you'll get in some track time, and when something else comes along, just go drive it.'

"Those first couple of days I was still just getting the engine put in. An oil fitting on the bottom that was made for the regular unblown Offy was stuck too far down and while Drake Engineering out in L.A. was making a different fitting for the oil line, Bobby was having to practice with the roadster's front end all raised up and jacked out of shape. But he liked it anyway. Somebody came up to him and asked him if he had a ride for the 500 and Bobby said, 'Sure I got a ride, that bastard right there. That's the sumbitch I'm driving.'

"Make a long story short, we made the show. And we never made it to the green flag. Got wadded against the wall right at the starting line with 11 other cars Then we barely got rebuilt in time for Milwaukee a week later, and Bobby had to run the 20-mile consie just to qualify for the 100-miler.

"Bobby was dead-ass last on the first lap and from then on was outrunning everybody and would have won but the chief mechanic fucked up. That's me! Trying to put the fucker back together after the crash at Indy, I forget about brake fluid, something I'd never done before in my life. And if I'd only have put a can of fluid in there and Bobby hadn't lost the brakes, he'd have been *gone*. We were handling good, and by then Bobby had had enough seat time to understand how to get the turbocharger up and running and keep [it] running.

"We ran some other races that season, and there was lots of experimental development and so forth. Right at the end of the year there was even a road race at Mount Fuji Speedway, Japan, that we went to. A turbocharged Offy roadster on a road course. Fuck! We might as well go have some fun!

"Bobby Grim was no road racer, but we were still running seventh, I think. And with one more bottom gear in that fucker, we'd have blown all of 'em off *bad*. There was a long downhill straightaway where Bobby was going by all those other sonsabitches at 180 or so, but then there was a 20-mile-per-hour hairpin where he had to turn around to go back up the hill. That's where we got fucked.

The roadster couldn't turn around and climb the hill, we didn't have a gear. . . ."

Herb sort of dried up after this, complaining that around this time "holes" in his security system mysteriously began opening up. And a lot of his turbocharging secrets got out and were incorporated by other teams working on turbocharging themselves.

Thanking Herb for everything, I excused myself. I knew he'd short-changed me on information about some of those other 1966 races where the Racing Associates 39 had competed, or perhaps he'd just forgotten about them. For recalling events four decades old, I thought he'd done well.

But later when I spoke with Bobby Grim to confirm Herb's version, I found Bobby's account so much more colorful and, occasionally, different that I'm including it for the record. Bobby was, for one thing, dumbfounded about Herb having accepted responsibility for the Racing Associates 39 losing its binders at Milwaukee. "*Herb* took

Herb Porter (standing, with stop watch) frowns, Bobby Grim grimaces, and the diabolical Racing Associates 39 turbocharged Offy lumbers onto the Speedway amidst the usual popping, slobbering, and hiccupping. *Indy 500 Photos*

the blame for that?" Bobby asked in quiet wonder. "I'm surprised. Everything else that happened with that turbocharger deal was always my fault."

Grim was an Indianapolis journeyman who drove in nine career 500s between 1959 and 1968, seven in roadsters. He was also one of the most dry-humored and deadpan funny drivers ever to break everybody up at the White Front. Sort of another Roger McCluskey.

"Everybody who ever worked for Herb Porter was either ready to quit or hit him in the head, you didn't know which," Bobby said, "and it was just Herb's way. No sense in taking it personal. Herb told you what was what and that was it. You didn't discuss things with Herb.

"Like, with his turbocharger, all the horsepower was set up so that it went on and off like a light bulb. No bottom end at all. An absolute plumber's nightmare of two sets of injector nozzles, one adjusted for unblown, the other for when the blower kicked in. Which meant that at low speeds the roadster was a slobbering idiot—pop, spit, slobber, it'd barely run at all. Then all of a sudden BLAM!, the turbo kicked in and it was hold-onto-your-ass.

"And what with all the spitting and slobbering, you had to nurse it, baby it, and burp it for three-quarters of a lap. Just to get everything cleared out. Well, I soon got fed up with that. So, this one time, I just lit 'er up to 8,200 in second gear on the pit road. Boy, that wasn't the answer."

"You cleared the pit road?" I asked.

"I cleared *everything*. Big black tire marks for a long ways. Everybody running."

Continuing, Bobby said, "I'd have killed to have a lower gear. But, no, Herb always went the other way: raise the gear, richen everything up. I was putting out maximum horsepower right at the end of the front and back straightaways, and naturally I tried talking Herb out of that. I told him we were making all our horsepower at the wrong end of the racetrack. We needed it when I was coming *off* the turn, not when I was already going way too fast getting *into* the turn. Everybody else in 1966 was going about 180, and somebody clocked me doing 200. Well, when you drive down into the corner already running 20 miles per hour faster than anybody else, the last thing you want is *more* power. But Herb never caught on to that. He was old school. He wanted maximum horsepower getting in, not coming off.

"Finally we qualified 31st, on the last row. Pole position on the wrong end. On the start, I didn't want any of that pop, spit, slobber business, so my foot was down and the turbo honking. But when everybody in front of me started wrecking each other, all those funny cars had the track blocked. I couldn't have gotten out of there with a helicopter. I hit the outside wall almost head-on and then backed the roadster's tail into the wall too. Two for one.

"Somehow the chassis hadn't been bent, and for Milwaukee Herb had the roadster's nose taped over and its broken tail chickenwired. We didn't have a clue what gear to run, and I think we ended up having to win a consie so we could start last in the 100-miler.

"And it was my day. You know how in a race the main pack breaks away into four or five lead cars, and then there'll be long gaps dividing the rest? Well, I worked my way up to one long gap, and then a yellow flag came out and I got to close it up for free. Four or five different times it happened that way, until I was just passing funny cars as I came to them. Nobody could see around that great big Watson, and if they tried getting me back around the outside, I'd just run 'em out of the groove. And anybody trying me on the inside took in the face a bolt of flame from the turbocharger, making them disappear immediately.

"I was popping, spitting, and slobbering like at the Speedway, but with the lower gear ratio and shorter racetrack, the turbo wasn't taking nearly as long to clear its throat. By halfway I was running around fourth, going faster than whoever was leading—Mario Andretti, I think. In my mind, I can still see him backing right up to me, but just then some of the cars I'd passed began repassing me because I started losing the brakes. I had to compensate by backing off the throttle early, and that killed the revs. I can't remember where I finished; somewhere in the top 10.

"We ran the rest of the pavement championship races, but the turbocharger was putting so much pressure on the magneto that the mag was always breaking down. All that summer we fought that mag. And when Herb finally got us a new one, my God, it was a whole new engine. Plus, things smoothed out a little when he got away from two sets of injector nozzles.

"At Trenton I was going right through the funny cars again, just like Milwaukee. But when this one funny car I was starting under changed its mind, I was coming way too fast to miss climbing over it and getting put out of the race. Herb thought the roadster had run out of brakes again, but it hadn't. Herb also used to holler about me getting tired and falling out of the seat. Actually I never did. I could drive that turbo all day long."

Bobby went on, "I suppose Herb told you how at the end of the season we went to some road race in Japan? The only thing that could be dumber than racing an offset Watson roadster on a road course was racing on a road course an offset Watson roadster that

Bobby Grim. *Indy 500 Photos*

was turbocharged. First of all came a bunch of sharp turns and hairpins—more pop, spit, slobber—and then there was this full U-turn right at the bottom of a long downhill straight. I just *loved* that one. One or two other turbocharged and supercharged Offys were over there, including Al Miller's funny car with a blown Offy. Early in the race its blower pitched, but Al went right on racing anyway, with about 90 horsepower. I caught up to him right in the middle of the U-turn, and there the two of us sat at about 20 miles per hour, staring at each other and popping and spitting and hiccupping and laughing like two idiots.

"By the end of 1966, I knew that a turbocharged Offy was going to become the way to go racing. And I knew that everything would really get going once the program got taken away from Herb Porter and turned over to somebody with common sense. Which is what finally happened. But give Herb a lot of credit. He was always experimenting with different turbocharger wheels, snails, intakes and exhausts. But what was really needed was somebody who wouldn't set up a turbo just to run fast at the end of a straightaway. And somebody who'd stick a gear in one and let the turbocharger wind up its revs and burn off all its fuel instead of wasting it. Other chief mechanics who were working with turbochargers were afraid to do anything to them at first, because Herb was the inventor and had all the answers."

I mentioned to Bobby the complaints Herb had about "holes in his security."

"Yeah," Bobby said, "and the funny thing was, I think that was Herb blaming me for something again. I don't know, but I imagine it was. And the truth was, I didn't know anything about turbocharger intakes and snails and stuff like that. And could have cared less. That was Herb's big project. The steering wheel was mine.

"What really happened wasn't a 'security leak' at all, just the usual White Front story. Herb'd go down there every night, get all gassed up, and then tell everybody what was what with turbochargers. I suppose

everybody in the White Front knew exactly what Herb was doing, and that meant everybody at Indianapolis knew."

I'd intended to share Bobby's testimony with Herb, give Herb the opportunity to rebut it if he wanted to, and then get back to Bobby and have him rebut Herb's rebuttals. But everything ground to a stop when Bobby's health suddenly began slipping and in 1995 he joined the growing number of roadster luminaries who have stepped off—Jud Phillips and Eddie Kuzma and Troy Ruttman and Larry Shinoda and Upside-Down Rounds and even Herb himself have since joined him.

Meanwhile, the Racing Associates 39 dinosaur and its mighty turbo Offenhauser is deserving of a worthy epitaph, and as "the father of the turbocharger," Herb had the best: "The fucker was one running son-of-a-bitch."

Here's why pit crews took the precaution of shrouding molten exhaust pipes in asbestos. Whoever in the 1963 500 was minding the dead man's switch on the Leader Card crew was asleep and A. J. Watson has his hands full with spurting raw methanol. *Indy 500 Photos*

Chapter 5
ATTACK ON SIGHT

So far everything I have presented about the Offy roadsters has been positive. But there is an opposing viewpoint which condemns them as "solid-axle race cars, wagon-sprung race cars, no-differential race cars, end-over-end and out-of-the-ball-park race cars." By any account, they were big, raucous, menacing machines that could dish out trophies or tombstones depending on the mettle, or the luck, of the men at the wheel.

Roadsters at Indianapolis took out Billy Vukovich, Manuel Ayulo, Keith Andrews, Pat O'Connor, Tony Bettenhausen, Jerry Unser—who survived an over-the-wall journey in 1958, but the following year couldn't survive a fire—and a rookie called Bob Cortner. At Trenton one got Jimmy Reece and at Milwaukee one got Smokey Elisian. Marshall Teague in a streamliner and George Amick in a lowbelly laydown bought the jackpot at Daytona. Roadsters got some good men.

Bad-behaving roadsters pitched some of the worst multivehicle tantrums ever seen at Indy. Just attempting to get lined up for the pace lap in 1957, a pair of Kurtis-Krafts sideswiped and slammed one another so hard they both had to abandon the proceedings on the spot. In 1959, four more Kurtis-Krafts met in the northwest corner, flipping one. In 1961, a copycat Watson ran amok at full speed when its oil tank broke open and began hemorrhaging along the front straightaway. Spinning out in its own slick, it kissed the wall and beached itself at the starting tower, where it instantly collected and disabled three other uprights and two laydowns. And in 1962, a Watson replica with a dynamite Offy motor was blowing off every enemy roadster in sight along the straights while behaving like a roadblock through the turns. A couple of impatient roadsters who

were jockeying to pass got sideways. A third roadster, a Kurtis-Kraft, slowed, but two imitation Watsons could not; and one of them slammed the Kurtis in the rump, flipping it over twice. The result: Four more roadsters knocked out of a 500.

In 1964, the Bardahl 86 was one of three Watsons and one Watson copy caught in a seven-car inferno that killed two drivers. The catastrophe started on the second lap in dense and fast-moving traffic when 1 of the 500's 11 funny cars torched its right-side fuel tanks against the front straightaway's inside wall, bounced back across the track a blazing wreck, and got T-boned by a second funny car. This fired the first funny car's remaining fuel tank.

Running like gangbusters into a solid wall of exploding gasoline three stories high came the Bardahl 86, the Clean Service Wear, the Leader Card Diet Cola, and the Hurst Floor Shift. The last three got stopped in time, but the Bardahl 86 couldn't; it had been positioned just behind the colliding funny cars.

Collecting a tire print across its nose, the Bardahl 86 roared underneath the flailing tail of the second funny car and straight into the raging fire. Climbing up over the top of the first funny car and almost into the cockpit of its driver, who may have still been alive, the Bardahl 86 somehow burst out of all the orange flame and black smoke into clear racetrack again. At that instant a four-wheel-drive STP Novi with its own steering gone smashed the Bardahl 86 in the hind quarters. This split open the Bardahl 86's full fuel tank without setting it on fire despite all the fire around it.

And the Bardahl 86—now trailing a fuel flood, and with the ruptured injector horns off the first funny car plugged into its undercarriage, along with the trademark lemon on a string that the driver of the second funny

Dick Rathmann and his chief mechanic Floyd Trevis watch as a spinning "Flintstone" prepares to wear out and "grow hair" prior to blowing out. Indy dinosaur chauffeurs tested strongly on self-preservation, and even throwing away a possible victory in the 500 didn't prevent them slowing down or pitting for fresh rubber when it was an emergency. It happened with the Bowes Seal Fast 8 in 1958 and during the war between the Bowes Seal Fast 1 and the Dean Van Lines in 1961. *Indy 500 Photos*

Opposite: All righteous disciples of the gospel of attack-on-sight: left to right (behind a sitting Rodger Ward), Troy Ruttman, Jim Rathmann, A. J. Foyt. *Indy 500 Photos*

car, Eddie Sachs, had liked to suck on, and with its own nose rubber smeared and its windscreen blackened and with the neck of its driver roasted to the second degree—the Bardahl 86 marched onward. It traveled around the first and second corners and the length of the backstraight before its driver, Johnny Rutherford, thought to stop and ask a fireman if he was burning. Told no, Johnny used the clutch to engage low gear and travel a little farther before at last parking the Bardahl 86 above a spreading ocean of methanol.

*N*othing but its split-open fuel tank was the matter with the Bardahl 86, and if its leak could have been patched during the 1-hour and 42-minute layover for the accident, then—in spite of all the horror he'd seen and barely survived—Johnny Rutherford was prepared to climb back into harness and return to the 500. Which may help explain why *Road & Track* magazine once categorized Johnny and other soldiers of the Offy roadster as stone-cold creatures who were "so brave it hurts to watch them."

R&T was and still is a sporty car book; its writers always thought the Indy 500 was a stupid race, and the description was meant as a put-down. Probably. Yet the magazine really was on to something without knowing it. A roadster wasn't an easy car to race, and not everyone was sufficiently "brave" to hot one through Indy's three and a half hours and 800 corners, or even through a 10-mile time trial. But if you were good enough, the roadster era was the very best time to be a race driver at Indianapolis. Never again have Brickyard champions been accorded more stature and respect.

Hanging on to control of an Offy roadster for 500 miles was interesting, to put it mildly, because Kuzmas, Epperlys, Lesovskys, Kurtis-Krafts, and Watsons all had their vices. None of them ever felt really "safe." Without baffles or screens to deflect or regulate the flow, a roadster had its handling go into the toilet when fully laiden with 450 pounds of methanol in its tail. Then enough burned off so that the weight was evenly distributed and a roadster came to its senses and briefly achieved a perfection of balance. But then, with the Indianapolis Motor Speedway glistening with thrown Meyer-Drake lubricant, and the corner groove going Firestone black, and its handling going loose, and its lap averages falling by 2 to 3 miles per hour, and its hard-shaking Offenhauser barking and vibrating in

complaint—then it was almost time for a roadster's first rehabilitating pit stop and the whole cycle to repeat itself.

Between 100 and 150 miles was as far as a roadster could travel before concluding its feast on its four quivering Firestones, especially the right rear, the traction tire. Going any farther without a pit stop was pushing it; a loud blowout followed by a long skid and slap-bang into the wall was next.

"Flintstones," the classically thin and tall Firestones were unfondly ridiculed, and they had weird tread patterns. Their dimensions were 8:00x18 rear; 7:60x16 front. On every sidewall in raised white letters were the words

FIRESTONE
Deluxe Champion
SAFETY-LOCK CORD
Gum-dipped

They were primitive and noisy. On any given day, a set could feel different, and they never felt good. It was like sitting on four rocks. More unsettling, chief mechanics used to walk drivers back to Gasoline Alley where they could study a worn-out Flintstone rotating on the rack at Bear Wheel Alignment. As the carcass started "growing hair," bright white canvas appeared, and the thought of that occurring at 170 miles per hour was enough to scare the bejesus out of all but the brainless.

Additionally, at least during practice sessions and time trials, the art of racing a roadster around Indianapolis was to chauffeur without using brakes. It was something new roadsters brought in.

Nothing available in those years was strong enough to whoa a fully loaded Offy roadster anyway, but weak and inefficient as roadster binders might be, traveling at Indy speeds without touching them at all was something else. Many drivers found it pretty tough going; however, the roadster drivers had no say in the matter, because the adage among chief mechanics was that if a roadster ever began burning out its brakes from overuse, you hired a different driver. And, for a driver, there was a defining moment when he found out whether or not he had it in him to race without brakes. Usually it happened when he was out taking his qualification time trial of four laps and was painfully aware that in order to make the show he had to reach and maintain an almost impossible mile-per-hour average. Amid an Offenhauser roar, and with his trimmed-out

---

Eddie Sachs had no mechanical faculty at all yet could put the Dean Van Lines on the ragged edge and hold it there at terrific speed. Once when he was out praticing with a "pushing" front end condition, he compensated for it by deliberately bouncing over a ripple in the track surface. It forced the Dean's rump to shift while his arms gave the steering wheel a sharp snap. *Bob Tronolone*

Jim Hurtubise gets his elbows out in the tall-tired Novi V-8, which he used to blow off Parnelli Jones on the first lap of the 500 of 1963. But three years earlier in 1960, in the Travelon Trailer, a Watson copy, "Hercules" had made his legend. Only a rookie, he ripped through his ten-mile time trial at a hair-raising 149.056, an astounding three miles per hour faster than the standing record; on one hurtling lap, he came within .399 of a mile per hour of breaking 150. People still talk about the run. Former chief mechanic Dave Laycock: "Basically, Hurtubise was keeping the roadster loose way on top of the race track, then making the four corners into two big corners. Running higher up going in, then not pinching it down and cutting off the revs coming off. He was the first guy to show 'em how to do that." *Bob Tronolone*

roadster humping along as fast as it could go, he came to the end of Indy's front or back straightaways at hurtling speed.

The job of slamming the great mother around turn 1 or turn 3 was at hand. Brave or not, no driver was enough of a nutcase to send his roadster lashing in there at 170 without lifting at all—that would croak him. Instead, the basic cornering drill of three steps, which evolved over time, mandated that a roadster pilot (1) "breath" his roaring Offy for a heartbeat (there'd be the trademark Offy BOOM as he came off the throttle) to permit his top speed to fall by no more than 30 miles per hour; (2) peel off still going so fast that maybe the driver's whole life was flashing before his eyes; and (3) right on the eye of the corner—and way, way before the driver really wanted to—righteously nail the throttle again to compel his careening roadster to "take a set."

Amazing things happened if a driver could carry out this drill, particularly if his marque of roadster happened to be a Watson.

Sixteen percent or more of its poundage was biased to the left, so when a Watson got "set" it was something like Clark Kent ripping off his suit and becoming Superman. The skeleton of chrome molybdenum gave a giant flex, all its weight shifted to the outside, and then the ever-lovin' Offy with its heavy flywheel and tall gear fired the whole works out of turn 1, up and across the short straight, and around turn 2. Then down the backstraight and bombing around 3 and 4, where the process repeated.

*S*o, do you follow? While Kuzma, Epperly, Lesovsky, Kurtis-Kraft, and Watson were busy throwing off all their roadsters, they were custom-tailoring them for a bunch of brave hombres who during Indy time trials could be depended on to avoid the brakes and mash the gas regardless of whether they wanted to or not. And who shared identical mind-sets when they were racing in the 500.

Bobby Marshman in the Econo Car Epperly, seventh fastest qualifier in 1963. Ordinarily, a Meyer-Drake had a throttle throw of roughly 2 inches. Before qualifying time trials, some drivers took the precaution of practicing with a throttle of 2 1/2 inches. Then, for time trials, they switched back to 2 inches. That way, while slamming down into turn one, they were lifting at the same number marker they had during practice. But when they gassed it, all the Offy horses cut in quicker. *Bob Tronolone*

Call it the mentality of attack-on-sight. Herb Porter, speaking like Herb Porter, explained the phenomenon best: "Those bastards were competitors—RACERS! When they saw another car, it was like they were thinking, 'Look, there's a race car there—I'm going to pass that son-of-a-bitch!' Roadster drivers worked off one another as stimuli. Whenever a couple of them got it on together, it was get-out-of-the-way."

Like everything else, the attack-on-site drivers came mainly from L.A. Eight of them won nine 500s in a dozen years. With space to reflect on just four of them, I'll begin with Pat Flaherty, the warrior saloon keeper with the go-to-hell mug on whom no less an eminence than Billy Vukovich bestowed a dandy nickname: Buffer Red.

Buffer Red

In July 1947, the Chicago fast-buck entrepreneur Anthony Granatelli created the Hurricane Racing Association. The razzle-dazzle Granatelli promotion style immediately made spectators go crazy and show up every week by the numbers at Soldier Field for the hot rod matches. Among many young hot-rodders heading out of L.A. to the Midwest to get in on the easy money was Pat Flaherty, a flame-haired Irish-American wearing a white helmet with a green shamrock for luck. He quickly discovered that the Hurricane bread wasn't so easy after all.

Hurricane races were so rampantly lawless they seemed straight out of the tradition of that other old Chi-town favorite, Scarface Al Capone. Among other things, every Soldier Field qualifying heat might contain a designated knock-off artist whose only assignment was to rack up any leader who was putting the grandstands to sleep winning in a runaway. There was T-boning, short-braking, cooked scoring counts, rooked results. Whenever conditions got tame in spite of all that, Andy Granatelli, as ringmaster, wasn't above dumping oil on the track. Essentially, the Hurricane Racing Association

Conventional dinosaur wisdom in emergencies held that when a roadster flew out of control its driver was supposed to turn left, say his prayers, and allow the monster to go wherever it wanted until it regained its senses. When he was an Indy rookie in 1961, Parnelli Jones said forget that. As if he were back racing a jalopy in Jalopy Derby, PJ fought the Agajanian Willard Battery for control, attained it, and in the process discovered a couple of things nobody else apparently knew. He discovered that allowing a dinosaur to slip and slide all over the place in the middle of a corner freed it up for the following straightaway. And while the Agajanian Willard Battery was in the spooky process of slipping and sliding, and its Flintstones were screaming and rolling and tucking under, Parnelli discovered he could develop fantastic momentum by nailing the throttle the instant the tall tires recoiled upright again. *Bob Tronolone*

functioned as a rough-and-ready academy, teaching Pat and a pair of other L.A. expates, Jim and Dick Rathmann—two future Indy 500 champions and one pole position winner—every dirty racing trick in the book.

Not that Pat at that time was harboring any strong Indianapolis ambitions anyway, no matter how big a deal the 500 was supposed to be. But in 1950, Pat came back for Memorial Day in a Granatelli heap that came in 10th. Both Rathmanns were in the 500 that season too. Like Pat, they already knew they could race and win anywhere and found Indy's long track and bricked surface unintimidating.

Unfortunately, what with their new Indianapolis licenses, any non–American Automobile Association racing that Pat and the Rathmanns did was punishable by suspension, and all of them were frequently banished from the three-A. One of Pat's blackballing's lasted for two years, meaning that he couldn't start in another 500 until 1953. And then another gap of two years occurred before he came back again in 1955. The explanation for the last gap was, partly, because he'd gone into the saloon-keeper business in Chicago. But also because Pat had had to spend time recovering from the effects of getting his bell rung in the brutal 500 of 1953.

The roadster evolution was really revving up that Memorial Day, with Vukovich's Fuel Injection Special and five similar low-silhouette Kurtis-Krafts in the field; the remaining 26 sleds, including Pat's, were the conventional lean and top-heavy upright champ dirt cars that the roadsters were in the process of putting out of business.

What a humane thing it was too. Reclining deep inside a low-hung roadster was a snap compared to the torture of spending 500 miles lashed to a tall dirt car. Sudden crosswinds along the backstraight made them nervous; but even worse was all the trauma their drivers absorbed straddling the driveshaft and riding the bricks out in the hot open air. Accordingly, 1953's 500 became one of the most humid and crippling on record, with 16 or 17 relief drivers having to substitute among 15 finishing cars; heat prostration followed by heart failure afterward got blamed for the demise of Carl Scarborough.

Jackhammering from 22nd to 5th in a minimal number of miles, Pat was putting on a rich display of the rough-and-tumble manners acquired courtesy of Hurricane rods. First getting mad and staving in his own nose drilling the deck of a slower car, Pat continued lapping faster than ever. Just as he seemed to be getting in his crosshairs the Fuel Injection Special—by then Pat was lapping as

Filling up the bottom groove, Flaherty and his Dunn Engineering, a barge of a Kurtis-Kraft, overwhelm the Peter Schmidt dirt track Kuzma and speed on to win 1955's Milwaukee 200. *Armin Krueger*

fast as Vookie was—Pat missed the northwest corner and caught its wall almost head-on. His accident was attributed to fumes, diplopia, and maybe old-fashioned Irish spirit. After spending the rest of the 500 miles staring at the long paint smear left from Flaherty's bright red car, Vukovich subsequently started calling Pat "Buffer Red," which stuck.

Recuperating from his skull fracture, Pat sat out much of the rest of 1953 and 1954 in Chicago tending bar at his own Windy City lounge. Then in the sad 500 of 1955 marked by the death of Vukovich, Pat started to bounce back, doing a remarkable job of coming in tenth—the final finisher to complete all 200 laps—with a no-account used Kurtis-Kraft dinosaur named, a touch ironically, the Dunn Engineering. Nobody today remembers this mechanical masterpiece very well, except for one old mechanic who described it to me as a "Big shitbox. Looked like the Mormon Wasp." Nonetheless, later that season on the flat Milwaukee mile where the summer 250-miler was second only to Indy in distance, the Dunn and Pat pulled off the monster upset of winning. And at almost the same time, 1955's Indy-winning trio of owner Jack Zink, chief mechanic A. J. Watson, and driver Bob Sweikert were disbanding.

Zink and Watson went to Pat expecting to recruit him for the 1956 500 where he could race the pink-and-white John Zink 8. It only seemed fair. Pat, after all, was a former citizen of Glendale, A. J.'s home; he and the Head were comrades from the Watson Dolly Company days. But Pat said no.

No matter how tempting the wheelhouse of the first Watson roadster might have sounded, all of Pat's loyalty was toward Dunn Engineering, the mom-and-pop team that had gotten him his first Indy car successes. Flattering telephone calls from Jack Zink and the Head couldn't budge Pat, but something else at last did: a pair of angry telephone calls from Glendale and his two loving older brothers Jim and John, crisply informing Pat that he was an idiot if he said no to such an opportunity.

Indianapolis, 1956, was marked by many things. The Speedway was resurfaced, the great majority of its original bricks done away with, and everything was smoother, faster, and trickier. A month of more rain than normal kept washing away whatever rubber got laid down in the groove. Practice was punctuated by 16 wrecks in 24 days. And Pat was on the verge of getting fired for his inability to bring the John Zink 8 up to speed.

Car and driver were not a good fit. The John Zink 8's 50-inch Halibrand axle was so stubby, and its right rear Flintstone tucked so

Twenty-five years old in 1963 when he passed his Indy rookie test, Johnny Rutherford, a three-time 500 champion of the future, afterward had to endure two agonizing weeks attempting to assure himself that the U.S. Equipment, a two-year-old Watson, would take a strong set and tolerate plenty of throttle. At last he successfully qualified at 148.063 miles per hour. "But that qualification run isn't what I remember best," Rutherford said in 1995. "The really big moment was the afternoon I finally just up and ran down into turn one without brakes, got the car all loose, then really got after the throttle. 'Whoa,' I said to myself. 'That worked.' I'd been almost six miles per hour off the pace; my averages looked like the pen got stuck on the paper—142, 142, 142. But this time when I got the board from the pit crew and my speed was way up, I was yelling 'I can do it, I can do it, I can do it!' Turn 1 the next time wasn't nearly as bad, and the lap after that was even better. Through repetition, I gained a tolerance. I was getting it. Getting brave." *Indy 500 Photos*

tightly to its coachwork, that a special cockpit shield already had had to be whipped up to protect Pat's right elbow. But the afore-mentioned new art-of driving an offset roadster, and particularly a Watson, was to negotiate corners by getting out of the throttle, stay-ing off the brakes, then getting back on the gas again at the right place. Jack Zink and the Head had run out of patience, chorusing, "Pat, please stay off the brakes!" So they dropped the "please."

All to no avail. Pat was of that first wave of Hurricane hot-rod racers who considered backing off early for any corner a humili-ating form of cowardice. Shut-off boards along Indy's front straightaway every 100 yards reading *3, 2, 1* were where Pat chose to celebrate and showcase his bravery by almost sailing clear past the *1* before jumping hard on the binders, which was about the

worst thing he could do. His heavy braking at the final instant was standing the John Zink 8 on its nose, throwing the chassis off bal-ance, killing momentum and lap speeds.

How it was that Pat at the last moment found the four miles per hour he needed and put the John Zink 8 on the pole position with new speed records depends on which of a pair of explanations you believe.

The one version has it that the John Zink team ordered Pat to get on the interstate and drive his passenger car to Chicago and back and not use the brakes, and that afterward Pat returned shak-ing and saying, "I almost killed myself nine times!" But at last he was ready to accept the technique.

The other explanation, one that a disgruntled Lindsey Hopkins went to his grave telling, had it that Jim Rathmann, who'd earlier

Pat Flaherty and the John Zink 8, the prototype Watson, set out on their very first practice run. "Buffer Red" is flat-mouthed and grim. Mechanics, spectators, and even a security cop all seem apprehensive. *Indy 500 Photos*

qualified the Hopkins Kurtis-Kraft on the Indy pole, got his brother Dick and the two Rathmanns next confronted Flaherty. Bad-mouthing their fellow Hurricane alumni as a gutless stroker for not being able to get the John Zink 8 going, the Rathmanns proceeded to throw him into a Gasoline Alley lavatory and wake up Pat by treating him to an ice-cold shower. Naturally enough, Pat lost his Irish temper over it and, still angry, proceeded to blow Jim Rathmann and Lindsey Hopkins right off the pole.

Wherever the truth lay, the 500 that followed was the craziest dinosaur Indy of all. Firestone was introducing a new and dubious tire and a lot of them blew out, helping put eight drivers into crash walls, including Dick Rathmann, who actually bit the cement after the finish, and four other unfortunates who met during a yellow caution. Mishaps nearly parked the second-, third-, fifth-, and sixth-place roadsters. One Kuzma invaded the pits to strike down a mechanic and break his leg; the longest period of sane racing between all the yellows was only 21 minutes; and Pat, whom not one of the usual experts had picked to win, did.

It was a fight all the way. The John Zink 8 got away late on the rolling start, so Pat overcompensated, messed up the first corner by getting in too hot, then fell behind three Kurtis-Krafts with half a dozen more at his back. One of them was a dorsal fin Novi Vespa, with all the usual Novi supercharged muscle, and Pat was wary of all Novis: inhaled Novi fumes had helped put him in cloud cuckoo land and into the wall back in 1953. Renewed trouble was coming in 1956. Just as Pat had caught up to the lead Kurtis-Krafts and was in the middle of a roaring duel with them, the Novi, too, at last got wound up and running. Catching up to the trio of Kurtis-Krafts and the John Zink 8 across the front straightaway, it nailed all four with one long and loud-screaming pass; the concussion was so severe that all dashboard gauges of the John Zink 8 temporarily went flat.

The first of the leaders to explode a Flintstone, the Novi next charged the southwest corner and crashed, and gradually the John Zink 8 got the upperhand on the remaining Kurtis-Krafts. Because Pat had asked for his right front Flintstone to be "really loaded," A. J. Watson had equipped him with an extra-thick Panhard rod, and the record-setting John Zink 8 was frequently observed with its inside front wheel spinning free of the track. Being "Buffer Red," Pat was flirting with walls and disaster by sometimes overtaking traffic high in the gray marbles and out of the groove. He never bumped into anybody as he had in 1953, but did get an opportunity to throw away the 500 with only minutes remaining.

Though the John Zink 8 had already lapped it 15 times, one of the defeated Kurtis-Krafts came to life once more and charged up from behind. Its driver, Tony Bettenhausen, buzzed and overtook. But instead of just letting Tony go, Pat decided to do the right thing and fight it out dinosaur driver–style. He'd just started around Bettenhausen on the outside again when a Flintstone on the Kurtis blew out and Bettenhausen—almost taking the John Zink 8 with him—backed into the wall and broke half a dozen ribs.

Upon taking the checkered in record time, a 3/8th-inch cross-strap on its throttle snapped in two, and Pat had to idle the John Zink 8 into Victory Circle. The IRS promptly helped itself to one-third of Pat's $37,527 share of the $93,819 winner's purse, and almost all of the remaining $25,000 and change went to cover hospital bills following Pat's big endo at the Springfield dirt track less than three months later.

Never the most physically strong or robust of dinosaur personalities anyway, he took his second long hiatus from Indy having his bones grafted. Missing the 1957 500, he was anticipating having his competition license restored in 1958, when he was supposed to be a member of a multidriver John Zink team. But three orthopedic surgeons examining his slow-healing fractures asked Pat to wait until 1959 to again represent Zink interests.

His John Zink 64 was the old John Zink 16 of 1958, one of that deadly 500's three front-row Watsons, and a roadster still rapid enough to win. Pat began business from deep in the pack. And his subsequent blast to the front became another of Herb Porter's "There's a race car there—I pass the SOB!" numbers. Jim Rathmann had started the 500 some 15 positions ahead on the front row, but after going around the inside and outside of a dozen roadsters in the first four laps Pat at 100 miles was already all over Jim fighting for the lead.

This was Pat's final 500. At 400 miles he was "Buffer Red" all over again and up against the wall with the John Zink 64's nose smashed and its fuel tank broken and dripping. Finding another dinosaur stopping in front of him, Pat took emergency action and swerved to the inside rail, then veered right and hit the outside wall and came to a stop facing the pit entrance. Supposedly he had been tiring but had refused to concede relief driver help. At least his wounds this last time were minor.

I hope that it's true but don't know if it really is: supposedly, during the John Zink 64's charge through six rows of traffic and momentarily into the lead, the Zink crew caught Pat being the first dinosaur driver to ever unofficially exceed 150 miles per hour.

Dick and Smokey

Anybody in 1958 who had a clue about what was going on was watching with anxious dread as the three Watsons occupying all of the front row—the McNamara Motor Express, the John Zink 5, and the John Zink 16—crowded down on one another into turn 3 at full screaming throttle on the 500's opening lap. This was one instance when *Road & Track* had it right: watching DID hurt.

The trio of Watsons had qualified one, two, three with Dick Rathmann on the pole with a new speed record for 10 miles; Smokey Elisian in the middle with a new speed record for one lap; and Jimmy Reece on the outside. And now with the back straightaway fast running out and turn 3 looming and somebody urgently needing to lift first, the question was, who would it be? Was it going to be Rathmann, who had a reputation for never doing so? Or would it be Elisian, who by some accounts had a death sentence hanging over his head from the Mafia and a mandate to lead or else? Or would nobody lift at all?

Dick and Smokey both did—but way, way too late. They collided. And the result was a savage and disastrous killer accident that might easily have taken out the whole field instead of only a quarter of it. Afterward, although Dick was getting some of the blame, the heaviest flak was falling on Smokey. And one thoroughly overwrought individual wanted A. J. Watson blamed too. But that individual happened to be old Frank Kurtis, whose five fastest Kurtis-Krafts had been eliminated by the crashing McNamara Motor Freight and John Zink 5, and who had a prior ax to grind with the Head anyway.

Ugly. Roadster racing wasn't always pretty, and what happened in 1958 was far from it. And yet somehow I can't stop marveling at the freaky and even scary chain of events and coincidences, set in motion through the years, that brought Dick and Smokey, arguably the two greatest carriers of the attack-on-sight dinosaur mentality going, crashing together at such a precise and calamitous moment.

In a poor neighborhood of Alhambra by the dry L.A. river—in whose cement bed Dick Rathmann used to get into rock fights as a 14-year-old—was where Dick and his canny younger bro, Jim, came from. "Dick" was born "Jim," and vice versa. They were a pair of prematurely bald and look-alike chrome domes who, upon first starting to race hot rods had agreed to exchange names so that "Jim" could get his underage license sooner.

"The big Rathmann" was how Dick came to be known throughout his roughhouse beginner years racing with his smallish brother and Pat Flaherty and their Hurricane 'rods. In addition to thickish shoulders and forearms, Dick had tattoos, a punch that could drop a mule, and an attitude. Teed off after the clunker he was driving survived barely 60 miles of the 1950 Indy, Dick's debutante 500, Dick decided to never race at the Speedway again and moved to the deep South to have NASCAR stock car adventures instead.

He raced bathtub Hudson Hornets and for several seasons was one of the best. At North Wilkesboro, a dirt track where dust hung so thick that Dick was still hacking it up an hour afterward, he held off all comers while racing and winning with a flat front tire. In one month he won races at Darlington, Langhorne, and Dayton, Ohio's high-bank short-track thriller—three of the most dangerous raceways on the planet. And when he wasn't having racing escapades, Dick was having traveling ones. In 1954, after competing one weekend at Atlanta, Georgia, he had six days to make it across the country to California and a meet at San Jose. Commuting via Chicago, he picked up another Hornet that had been in a rollover and spent three sleepless nights in a garage straightening it, then set out towing to the Pacific Coast in a blizzard. The transmission of his Lincoln tow car broke and Dick arrived at San Jose pulling the Lincoln behind the Hudson! During warm-ups its gas tank fell out onto the racetrack. Dick asked one of the other, slower, Hornet drivers to loan him his gas tank and was refused. So Dick took it from him anyway. He won the race, got protested by a runner-up Oldsmobile driver, then won again on appeal.

On May 1, 1955, the death at Langhorne of Mike Nazaruk indirectly returned Dick to Indianapolis. The ex-leatherneck Nazaruk had been the favorite driver and frantic carousing companion of good-time Lee Elkins, the full-on boss of McNamara Motor Freight and its Indy team. Elkins was in mourning for Nazaruk for almost a year. And then, needing a replacement for the McNamara Kurtis-Kraft, Elkins, who still liked his race driver employees to be larger than life, just like himself, chose Dick as Nazaruk's logical replacement.

Together they did the crazy 500 of 1956. It was the May of Pat Flaherty's victory, and also the May when Dick and Jim supposedly had to heave Pat into an icy shower to get him mad enough to qualify. And it was the May when eight of the 500's dinosaurs went into walls, including Dick's.

Dick got away unharmed, but Lee Elkins didn't get the Kurtis repaired in time so Dick, swinging his *cojones* around, sought a new ride for the 1957 500 elsewhere and immediately found one. He put the Sumar, a Kurtis-Kraft, in the show, then for reasons having nothing to do with his driving had to relinquish it. Just a few nights before the race he got into a brawl in front of a whorehouse on back-street Indianapolis and it took 14 stitches to repair one of his eyes. Dick still managed to distinguish himself. By passing the month taking test hops in various dinosaurs, he established new standards for bombing in deeper, jumping off the brakes later, yet still somehow being able to get back on the gas faster than anybody else. Afterward the quaint old dinosaur driver term of somebody being "Braver than Dick Tracy" was judged obsolete; "Braver than Dick Rathmann" went into wide usage.

The following year, 1958, all of the chance happenings and ominous coincidences that impacted the 500 and turned it into the disaster it was started kicking in almost as soon as May began.

First, A. J. Watson arrived from Glendale with his three John Zinks, the Nos. 5, 16, and 44, as well as the unpainted, engineless No. 97 that he'd constructed for the purpose of selling. Next, Lee Elkins—seeing No. 97's "for sale" sign and wanting to make up for McNamara Motor Freight not having an entry for Dick the previous year—stepped up and sponsored it. Time was passing. Practice was starting, and all that Elkins and Dick had was their unpainted Watson, no engine, and no garage in Gasoline Alley. Somehow it all worked out. The silver-and-red McNamara livery and lettering got thrown on so hastily that Dick's name on the flanks came out *Rathman*. The gofer whom Elkins dispatched to the McNamara headquarters in Kalamazoo made it back with an Offenhauser overnight. A den in Gasoline Alley so bare bones it lacked even a workbench opened up. Floyd Trevis, the builder and sometime-

Buffer Red's big moment in Victory Circle at the Speedway was followed only 11 days later by another big one in the winner's circle on the Milwaukee mile. But a harsh reckoning was awaiting on the Illinois State Fairgrounds at Springfield later that summer. *Mike Flaherty collection*

chief, became available to preen No. 97 and immediately began pressing Watson in the Zink garage for information about how a Watson roadster worked.

All this time, Dick had been impatiently pacing up and down, hot to trot to get out on the Speedway. Just 42 miles worth of practice and one spinout along the pit road later, he was above 146 miles per hour and going faster than anybody else with one exception. Unfortunately for all concerned, that exception happened to be Smokey Elisian.

If he were still with us, "Smokey" wouldn't like me calling him that. He would probably say, "Screw you. The name's Ed." "Smokey" was the sobriquet his master Billy Vukovich had given him, and only Vookie was permitted to use it.

"I still don't think people know what to make of me," Ed/Smokey admitted in a 1959 letter to his parents only a month or so before his death. "I mean, unless they actually meet me in person, I must be the very bad! bad! so-and-so they have read so much about." And Smokey was right; a lot of people did think he was "bad." Not by nature friendly anyway, his burly physique and swarthy complexion seemed vaguely menacing, as did his confusing, introverted personality and mournful eyes. There was furthermore the scandal of his gambling, and the crucial role he shared with Dick Rathmann in bringing on what was the dinosaur Indy's worst accident. So all this made Smokey a villain; and to some a villain is what he has posthumously remained. Maybe he deserves to be. And yet . . .

As I compose this, I stare at a picture of Smokey, a photograph of him snapped right after he'd completed "Ed Elisian's Midnight Run," one of the lesser burlesques of the 500 of 1955. Final qualifications had closed down with Smokey, who'd gotten a bad call from the chief steward Harry McQuinn on his first attempt, being denied a second chance. So J. C. Agajanian, using his clout, stood tall for a fellow Armenian and declared that he'd withdraw his own entry unless Smokey got a second shot. Whereupon Smokey proceeded to successfully requalify under late-afternoon skies so dark that one of his mechanics celebrated the occasion by posing for the picture holding a hurricane lamp. But here's the thing: mechanics and other drivers in the photo are whooping it up and celebrating the excellence of Smokey's accomplishment, and Smokey himself is the only guy not laughing or at least grinning. I have never, ever, seen a picture of him doing that, and I believe I know why.

Some years back, for reasons I never completely understood, my own personality and hold on life began deteriorating. And in a matter of weeks I'd spiraled into a state of utter despair and self-loathing. Just dragging myself out of bed some mornings became an accomplishment. And it turned out I had turned into that one tortured American out of five who had gotten laid low by clinical depression. Various psychiatrists, different medications, and mainly the bedrock support of family and friends brought me around again, but it was a terribly painful haul. Depression's causes and effects are still not fully understood as we head into the next century; in the fifties they were hardly acknowledged. Smokey Elisian, I believe, was a chronic sufferer of this terrible affliction, yet never had access to the shrinks or magic potions to bail him out of it. I don't suppose he ever realized what was wrong. Maybe that does not excuse all the dumb things he did, but for me it helps explain them.

Unlike Pat Flaherty and Dick Rathmann, Smokey wasn't a product of L.A. but of San Francisco, which in the late forties had an almost equally strong hot-rod scene. The 500 of 1954 was Elisian's first, and he didn't do well, requiring the assistance of a relief driver. Later that same year he got all beat up in a sprint car spill at Fort Wayne, Indiana, and afterward accepted a lift home to the coast from Billy Vukovich, in the Dodge pace car Vookie had won at the 500.

All dinosaur drivers admired Vookie; Smokey, what with the special nickname Vukovich had given him and all, worshipped him. In return he got needled and verbally abused the same way that Vukovich gave it to everyone else, but that didn't stop Smokey from aping his idol's most vivid mannerisms, including walking around glaring and squeezing hard rubber balls with both hands. Vukovich's 1955 demise left Smokey bereft, and perhaps this was when depression began biting him. He remained in so much despair that he never made it to the Victory Banquet to receive a sportsmanship award for having spun his own car out of the 500 to try and rescue the dead Vookie from his crashed and flaming Lindsey Hopkins Kurtis-Kraft.

A. J. Watson always had a weakness for hairpin employees—he had Fat Boy Ewing as his tin man, remember—plus he enjoyed giving hard-up drivers a hand. In 1956, with its victory at Indy, the John Zink team of Watson, Jack Zink, and Pat Flaherty and the John Zink 8 was riding high. So, for a 200-miler at Darlington, Watson got the nod from Jack Zink to have Smokey put on Zink pinstripes and race a second Zink machine, the team's upright dirt tracker. It was the same automobile in which Flaherty subsequently suffered debilitating injuries at Springfield, but at Darlington Smokey did a good job of bringing it in fifth, just behind Flaherty in the John Zink 8. With Flaherty hurt, the Zink team was suddenly down to one chauffeur, Smokey, so following Springfield Watson repaired the upright for Smokey to race in a no-points curiosity show on Dayton Speedway's high-pitched half. It became the only championship meet Smokey ever won, and afterward he looked as confused and mournful as ever.

Difficult as it was for a driver to get into the Head's doghouse, Smokey managed it at the next race. It was 250 miles around Milwaukee, and what happened might have been pathetic had it not also been so painfully comic.

Continuing to experiment with different drivers, Watson had Dick Rathmann in the John Zink 8, Smokey back in the upright. He got in only as an alternate starter, but once the race began the

continued on page 129

Dick Rathmann & tattoos got this first A.J. Watson crate up to 131 miles per hour in 1950, fast enough to qualify for the year's 500. Mingled amidst other members of the ecstatic, and perhaps stunned, pit crew are Watson and Jim Rathmann; Dick's buddy Buffer Red leans on the tail. *Tower Photographers, Scalzo collection*

"What the hell was THAT about?!" Dick Rathmann says he yelled to Smokey Elisian, as the pair of them scrambled uninjured from their broken McNamara 97 and John Zink 5. They had crashed into turn 3's outer wall, taking a quarter of 1958's starting field with them. *Indy 500 Photos*

Continued from page 122

attack-on-sight mentality kicked in hard as ever: In 7 miles Smokey passed a dozen cars and went from 26th to 14th. Next he bumped into two other cars, got black-flagged, but was permitted to rejoin the race.

Then the laugh-riot began. To get a stronger grip of the wheel, Smokey, prior to the start, had wrapped it with the contents of a 200-foot roll of friction tape. And during one of the yellows he observed that the tape was unwinding and began rewrapping it. But he couldn't complete the job before the green came out again. So, with loose tape billowing all through the cockpit, Smokey raced along awaiting another yellow, whereupon he got busy wrapping again.

Watson noticed him doing it and had Larry Shinoda give him a pit board ordering him to stop and concentrate on the race. All Larry could think to write was "Quit It." Smokey ignored the board and continued wrapping. Larry lost his patience and gave him the finger. Smokey gave him the finger back. This situation continued through the 154th mile when Smokey—still steering, wrapping, and flipping off Larry—lost his concentration and backed into the south turn fence, where the fuel tank split and a flash fire started up.

When the John Zink team pulled out of Milwaukee that night, it left Smokey behind.

Playing amateur witch doctor, I think this may have been when Smokey's mental state took another turn for the worse. Whose wouldn't? He looked up to Watson almost as much as he had Vukovich and now Watson had decommissioned him. Smokey, apparently, was already a gambler of long-standing, but the next year, 1957, he became a compulsive and self-destructive one. Whether it was getting into day-and-night poker marathons for high stakes in the casinos of Las Vegas or Reno, or just pitching pennies in dives, he couldn't or wouldn't make himself stop. In Chicago some professional gamblers pointed a gun at him, and this

Despite getting blamed for the destruction of half a dozen fellow roadsters, and the death of Pat O'Connor, all wounds to the John Zink 5 were minor: one small kink in the frame, a bent tailpipe, and a lost grill. Had its Offenhauser not stalled out, it might have been capable of continuing in the 500. Once repaired, the John Zink didn't sit idle for long. Thirty days after the 500 disaster, it was shipped to Italy and the Race of Two Worlds at Monza. Its winning average of 166.73 miles per hour bettered a long-standing international close-course speed record. Back in the United States again, it sat on Milwaukee's pole position, led 13 of the 200 miles, then spun out of second place at 125 miles. A year later, at Trenton in September of 1959, it crashed practicing and absorbed heavy nose and tail trauma. It sat parked through 1960. In 1961, painted candy apple purple with gold trim and re-named the Denver-Chicago Trucking, it was one lap away from qualifying for the 500 when it pitched its engine. Five years and much history old, yet still not decrepit, in 1962 it succeeded in out-qualifying half the Indy starting field but detonated a piston at 32 miles. *Indy 500 Photos*

was when the rumor started at the 1958 Indy that the Mafia itself was after him.

But other things were occurring in 1958. Originally envisioning a three-dinosaur entry, the John Zink team was in chaos. Pat Flaherty was supposed to have been in the new John Zink 16, Troy Ruttman the year-old Zink 5, and either Jimmy Reece or Jud Larson the John Zink 44. But Flaherty couldn't pass his physical, and Ruttman was driving for J. C. Agajanian. So Reece got re-assigned to the Zink 16 and Larson remained in the Zink 44. And A. J., who still had a soft spot for Smokey, and respect for his throttle foot, assigned him the Zink 5.

Jud Larson was a dirt track icon who didn't like racing on anything but dirt. Jimmy Reece was an Okie crony of Jack Zink's who'd made a career of being a coast-and-collect merchant. Not using any brakes felt so unnatural to him that the Zink team took the precaution of rigging up to the Zink 16's cockpit a second brake pedal made out of wood. And then Jimmy was informed that whenever he took the Zink 16 so deep into turn 1 that it scared him, he had permission to push the bogus wooden pedal instead of the real thing. Jimmy named it the "Oh, Jesus!" bar—the first words that came to him when he tried it.

Smokey, then, was the Zink team's unlikely new leader. Never in his career had he ever had a race car like the John Zink 5 under him, and his speeds shook everybody up. By Wednesday afternoon, two days before time trials, he was hammering the Brickyard at 146.914, unofficially quicker than Flaherty's standing records.

Until Dick Rathmann made his own dramatic appearance in the McNamara Motor Freight, Smokey had the glory to himself. Then on Friday morning Dick went out for only his second shakedown cruise in the McNamara and got above 147—so delighting Lee Elkins, Floyd Trevis, and the entire McNamara crew that everybody took the rest of the afternoon off and adjourned to the White Front.

The John Zink 5 was back inside its garage being worked on with its hood open when Smokey arrived, distraught at now being only second fastest, and ordering all the Zink mechanics to close the hood NOW because he was going to go out and blow off Dick's speed. Lapping at 144, then 145.148, he concluded the three-lap binge with a how'd-ya-like-that? 148.148.

All speeds were down the next day when it was official, but Smokey still managed to clock the top lap of time trials, 146.508. And Dick in the McNamara Motor Freight won the pole position by exploding Flaherty's four-lap speed record with a 10-mile run of 145.974.

Smokey and Dick were the two drivers destined to bring on the most ghastly wreck of roadster Indy, yet off the track got along famously. They were even lodged together in the same flophouse dormitory, a downtown Indianapolis institution of clean living called the YMCA. Still, there were extremely bad vibrations about what was going to happen come Memorial Day when they both got it on. Another "Smokey"—Smokey Yunick—thought he overheard Elisian saying that if he led the 500's opening lap it would settle all his gambling worries, causing Yunick to conclude that Smokey must have had an enormous wager riding on it. Pat O'Connor, starting on the second row, had a nervous conversation with Paul Russo and expressed concern about what type of agenda Dick and Smokey might be planning directly in front of him. The writer Angelo Angelopolus quoted A. J. Watson as saying the Zink team was starting Smokey on scuffed Flintstones and only a half-laden tank because they expected him to go for it early. And on the morning of the 500 Dick claimed that Smokey arrived with the veins of his neck throbbing with anticipation and intensity, plus chain-smoking when he was normally a nonsmoker.

Matters were exacerbated even further by Indy's ongoing experiments with confusing new starting systems. Instead of being marshaled along the front straightaway as usual, everybody was lined up single file along the pit lane. The first roadster to move onto the track was Dick's McNamara Motor Freight, then Smokey's John Zink 5, and then Jimmy Reece's John Zink 16—the front row. But somehow the pace car emerged next, followed by the rest of the field. So, when the front row came past the starting line all by itself and well ahead of everybody else, the starter had to vigorously flag Dick, Smokey, and Jimmy to catch up. Dodging and weaving their ways through 10 rows of dinosaurs, the trio didn't become aligned in position until they were crowded together on the northwest corner coming WFO for the green.

It was a ragged start. Dick led around corners 1 and 2 and then down the backstraight toward the third corner. Arriving there going 170, he had Smokey on his inside elbow also coming at 170. Throughout the month, the two had always practiced by themselves and never confronted one another on the track. But now it was roadster bravery versus roadster attack-on-sight mentality. The result was that the McNamara Motor Freight and the John Zink 5 were well past the point of crashing before Dick or Smokey would consent to lift. And by then the John Zink 5 and the McNamara Motor Freight both got sideways and began sliding backward across the groove.

And while the two of them were busying wrecking one another, along came the John Zink 16 and Jimmy Reece to finish the job. Locking up its brakes in the middle of the racing groove and plugging up the track, Jimmy's John Zink 16 got rammed from the back, whereupon other roadsters also began exchanging body blows, including Pat O'Connor's Sumar, which tipped over. And then Indy burst its seams with skidding, bashing, out-of control roadsters until the demolition finished with O'Connor dead, Jerry Unser in the McKay Kurtis-Kraft over the wall, and the 500 emptied of seven of its drivers, including Dick and Smokey.

Smokey's great opportunity had deteriorated into Smokey's great disaster—"Fuck, it's the story of my life," he was heard to mumble bitterly—and everybody wanted him punished.

"For the safety and well-being of himself and his competitors," the U.S. Auto Club first tried pulling his competition license, but chickened out from blaming Smokey alone for the melee. Still

wanting to hammer him, the sanctioning body next did an investigation and discovered that, lo and behold, Smokey had been commuting around city boulevards with a suspended driver's license. Grounding him from racing on the strength of that, however, was just too vast a stretch. No roadster driver was so saintly that he wasn't hell-on-wheels on the streets—including Rodger Ward, the most discreet of the lot, who'd once lost his license for racking up as many citations as Smokey. So at last the U.S. Auto Club used the notoriety of Smokey's gambling debts to kick him out.

Smokey went home to California, got in more hot water for passing a hot check, then was in and out of the clink for failure to report for fingerprinting to the probation office. Broke, he agreed to engage in more speed wars. Against Dick!

In what became a series of hippodrome freak shows, Smokey and Dick climbed into some rag-top late-models and were instructed to make like pro 'rasslers having a grudge match. The rag-tops they raced, and the backwater tracks where they raced them, looked more precarious than roadsters and Indy itself. All the debasing hype and hokum at last wore out in West Memphis, Arkansas, where Smokey and Dick and the race promoter almost had to sell the freak show promoter's Caddy to raise funds to get out of town. And when Smokey returned to the Bay Area he got landed on by marshals who extradited him back to Indiana on still more bad check charges. Released again, he returned to the coast and went to work doing everything from driving dump trucks to working at his brother Al's rug business. And he continued wondering how he was ever going to satisfy all the hard gambling characters who had him in hock.

Gambling is reputed to be the hardest vice to eradicate, worse than booze. Somehow, Smokey managed it. Impressed, the likes of Watson and Thomas Binford, president of the U.S. Auto Club, kicked in a couple of thousand apiece to settle Smokey's debts.

Meantime, back at Indy were car owners, chief mechanics, and especially drivers who remembered the 1958 500 and lived in fear of Smokey being reinstated to race at Indianapolis again, ever. But Smokey still was Indy's one lap record holder, he'd gone faster in a roadster and come closer to the vaunted one minute lap than anybody else and had even told Dean Van Lines that if the team ordered him a new Watson dinosaur for 1960 he'd simultaneously beat 150 and set it on the pole. Believing Smokey, Dean was having one tooled up by Fat Boy Ewing (Eddie Sachs instead of Smokey would make it famous). Everything was going better now and, judging from a letter to his parents, so was Smokey's depression: "I have gained some esteem and self-respect over the past few months and I seem to gain more every day. . . . I do have so much to live and look forward to!"

Sadly, but inevitably, Smokey's days as a reformed man would be few. On August 30, 1959, his ride at Milwaukee, the Travelon Trailer, a Watson copy which later made the headlines with Jim Hurtubise, hit an oil slick on the 29th mile and got upside-down and on fire. Smokey burned to death.

Smokey Elisian, A. J. Watson, and Jack Zink. Following the big crash, a national magazine published a picture of Smokey, head in hands, slumped on the pit wall. "The story of my life," he complained. "Don't worry about it," the Head consoled, "we came to race." And to those who continued jumping up and down on Smokey, Watson, with an unusual burst of temper, snapped, "Listen. They fire you around here for not driving hungry." *Indy 500 Photos*

Following pages: Milwaukee, summer of 1959. The Travelon Trailer, Smokey's last ride, got repainted pink, pearl, and purple for the 1960 Indy 500. Then its new, not-of-this-planet freshman pilot, Jim Hurtubise, who didn't mind getting way out of shape and loose in the corners, gunned it to within a blink of 150 miles per hour. *Armin Krueger*

As for Dick Rathmann, he did another five 500s from 1959 through 1964, and in 1961 had a brief and exciting flirtation with one of the Novis that could have, but didn't, result in the big one-five-oh lap. Yet without having Smokey around pushing and inspiring him, Dick hardly seemed the same driver.

The collision of Smokey Elisian and Dick Rathmann, the death of Pat O'Connor and the out-of-the-ball-park ride of Jerry Unser, the near wipeout of a quarter of the field, the rumor of Mafia gambling debts, plus all the accompanying emotions of fear, bravery, grief, anger, and blame led to Memorial Day 1958 being the most dramatic moment of all roadster 500s.

Rodger

Rodger Ward owns the distinction of winning the most roadster races, 11, including 2 Indy 500s. Not only was he the indisputable master of the Watson roadster but, along with Watson, arguably the one indispensable Offy roadster personality.

Rodger was one of the older drivers, but he could blow off old and young alike. He outlasted (and outlived) his peer Shorty Templeman in 1962; the same year, he outsped Templeman's hotshot replacement, Jimmy McElreath.

Shorty was one of the tiniest chauffeurs to ever hang on to a roadster—all 5 feet and 40-something rugged years of him. Before coming to dinosaurs he'd been a celebrity champion of 110 Offy midgets, and he still raced the mean little buzzbombs as a way of staying fighting fit.

Shorty never had much money, and over the 1961 winter was working at a northside Indianapolis gas station where a car slipped off its jack and mashed his leg. He showed up at the Speedway the following May limping, but tough-as-nails as ever, even though he still didn't have any money and had to spend the month sleeping in his station wagon out on the parking lot behind Gasoline Alley. His roadster was the Bill Forbes Watson. Starting up front, Shorty touched another roadster, or perhaps the wall, with sufficient wallop to rupture the sway bar anchor to the front axle. This, in turn, set off nasty misalignments up and down the roadster steering chain, which Shorty fought for 500 miles, still finishing a hauling-ass 11th. But it wasn't good enough, and after an even worse Milwaukee, Shorty suffered the fate of all nonperforming dinosaur drivers and got fired. Down on his luck even more than he realized, he went midget racing in Ohio and ate it in a crash.

The driver who replaced Shorty in the Bill Forbes was another extreme case, Jimmy McElreath, a racing bricklayer out of cowboy Arlington, Texas. Big Jimmy had all the worthy background ingredients demanded of an Offy roadster driver, including great anecdotes. One time he and a buddy had visited a friendly honky-tonk cowboy bar to hit on some of the cowgirls when one of the cowgirls' boyfriends objected and pulled and fired his piece. And Jimmy ended up taking lead in the ankle from the same pill that first pierced his buddy's butt.

Jimmy made his reputation and earned Rookie of the Year honors in the 1962 500, mostly on the strength of one bold maneuver.

Standing on the gas of a hodgepodge of an old Kurtis-Kraft with a Watson front end, he'd come recklessly storming down into turn 1 and proceeded to overtake both of A. J. Watson's Leader Card team cars as he came to them, getting the Leader Card 7 coming in and the Leader Card 3 coming off. Still full of racing and savoring the memory at the awards banquet, Jimmy asked the audience, "What'd Watson think when I blew off both his boys?"

He was referring in part to Len Sutton, the Leader Card 7's journeyman chauffeur, who was the 1962 500's runner-up. But Jimmy was presumably having even more fun giving both barrels to Rodger Ward, the pilot of the Leader Card 3 and the 500's winner. Rodger was already well accustomed to getting dissed and being underrated; he took such comments in stride.

Rodger originally came out of L.A., like everyone else. He wasn't, however, a hot-rod driver but a graduate of postwar Gilmore Stadium and its tricked-out midgets—Rodger was the only junkyard Ford V-8-60 pilot to ever upend all of Gilmore's pedigree Offys. But for several seasons afterward Rodger's Indy car career was on the skids. First he got caught in the middle of the 1954 pileup at Du Quoin that killed the eminent chief mechanic Clay Smith. And then in 1955 at Indy, Rodger's doggy Aristo Blue Kuzma was one of the unholy trio of crashing dirt cars and roadsters that brought on the demise of the godly Vukovich.

For several seasons afterward, Rodger felt almost as ostracized as Smokey Elisian had. Yet how he coped with it was odd. Instead of making amends, he went out of his way to behave badly; the drinking race driver was somewhat in vogue anyway, but he took it to extremes.

The best thing yet to happen to Rodger was his 1957–1958 association with Herb Porter, chief of car owner Roger Wolcott's outfit. Rodger and Herb won five dirt and pavement championship races together, including two Milwaukees and one at Trenton with Herb's "bent engine eight ball," the Wolcott Fuel Injection No. 8 roadster created in collaboration by Lujie Lesovsky and Herb.

Expecting his fair share of the credit for this as he did with everything else, Herb once said that not only did he save Rodger from a life of drunkenness, but additionally he taught him how to race a roadster. "See," Herb explained to me, "I was the one who showed Ward how to get around a paved track. We were up at Milwaukee, and after practice he told me, 'Goddamn, boss, I'm lost!' So I walked him down to the first corner to look at the other drivers. 'If you think you're in trouble,' I said to him, 'just look at them assholes. All over the fuckin' place.' And they were. 'You'll be just fine,' I told him.

"The philosophy I preached to all my drivers on a mile track was that once they put their own left front wheel in front of or next

---

Rodger Ward's first ride in a Watson at Indy in 1959 also resulted in Rodger's first 500 win. In 1962 he added a second. And in 1960 he was second, in 1961 third, and in 1963 fourth. *Indy 500 Photos*

THE INDIANAPOLIS NEWS

WARD WINS THE '500'

4th EXTRA

Lap-by-Lap Story of 500-Mile Race

More attack-on-sight. Ward goes after Foyt. *Indy 500 Photos*

Previous pages: Gargantuan as his roadsters appeared to be, A. J. Watson somehow managed to make one weigh less than a Kurtis-Kraft, Lesovsky, Epperly, or Kuzma. The Head was always on a lightweight kick. Basically, though, he seldom experimented or much changed his formula, except in 1961 when he dramatically saved an additional 200 pounds by replacing torsion bars with coil springs, and by reducing the diameter of the chrome moly skeletons of the Leader Card 41 and the Sun City. In the aftermath, the Head judged the Sun City his mistake roadster, "the worst one I ever built." And Rodger Ward, who drove the Sun City, and had had input in its design, agreed: "Me thinking I was smart enough to help Watson design a car—how dumb can you be?" Yet the Sun City really wasn't that bad. It led seven laps of the 1961 500, set a track record for 400 miles, and came in third; five days afterward it won at Milwaukee, leading all 100 miles. And at Trenton later that fall and following spring, the Sun City twice came in third. Watson, however, gave up on coil springs. And after converting back to torsion bars, he and Rodger promptly won the 1962 Indy with the Leader Card 3. *Indy 500 Photos*

to the other asshole's front wheel, they'd just taken over the other asshole's throttle. Ward qualified back on the fifth row, so I told him, 'Here's what we're going to do. First get squared away. And then going into the first corner just start driving by those sonsofbitches on the outside.' We won the race. I stood there in the pits all day long, watching the top of Ward's helmet going around all those bastards on the outside." But then Roger Wolcott died unexpectedly at the end of 1958, the team folded, and Rodger sensed things starting to go sour for him all over again.

Jim Rathmann and George Amick were two other drivers searching for employment at the beginning of 1959, both hoping to find it at Leader Card, the new roadster team of Bob Wilke and A. J. Watson. Rodger thought he belonged at Leader Card himself, but every attempt he made was rebuffed. First Wilke told him that Leader Card was hiring Rathmann, but then Rodger heard via the grapevine that Rathmann was staying with Lindsey Hopkins. This time when Rodger telephoned Wilke, the car owner told him he was hiring Amick. Then word came that Amick was going to race for George Bignotti and Bowes Seal Fast. So Rodger called Wilke a third time, they had a meeting in L.A., and out of this came roadster racing's great "three Ws" trinity—Wilke, Watson, and Ward.

They went to Daytona Beach together for 1959's opener. Rodger was running second in the Leader Card 5, his first Watson roadster, thinking it was the fastest race car he'd ever sat in—"And then I spun that turkey out" and touched the wall. That was an inauspicious way to begin, but it was the last time Rodger—who ended up racing more of them than anyone else—ever put a scratch on a Watson. Racing with great savvy the Leader Card 5, the Leader Card 1, the Sun City, the Leader Card 3, and the Kaiser Aluminum—five

different Watsons in five years—Rodger became A. J. Watson's boy, and together their 1959–1963 Indy 500 finishing record—first, second, third, first, and fourth—is unequaled in the dinosaur era.

Rodger was nearly the only thing that the proud but lethal fifties had left to throw at the sixties. And the new decade's young roadster heroes—Foyt, Jones, Hurtubise, Rutherford, and the 1962 Rookie of the Year, Jimmy McElreath—were cheeky enough to call Ward "the old man" to his face. Their youthful faces said "race drivers," where Rodger's middle-aged one said "clerk." But there was never anything remotely geezer-looking about Ward while he was celebrating and kissing all the girls in Victory Circle with Flintstone waste and Offenhauser oil filth plastered all over his seasoned mug, particularly after he'd just stuffed the young punks for yet another 500 win.

"Leader Card's was just a great team, and driving a Watson roadster was a pleasure," Rodger said once, "but what primarily gave me so much confidence in the overall team was because A. J. was always better at determining what I needed than I was. We'd arrived at the Speedway always coming to race, and whatever vintage Watson roadster we had always ran great, but sometimes I couldn't relate to A. J. about what the car was doing that I didn't like. So sometimes I'd say, 'Well, I'm kind of confused,' and Watson would watch me practice again and then say, 'I want to try something. Kind of watch your ass for a few laps and give me your opinion.' And nine times out of ten what he'd done had fixed the problem."

With all the words I've laid down about brave drivers, aggressive drivers, and fighting drivers, it's mystifying that the most successful Offy roadster driver of all was the one who was the most preservation-minded, the one who crafted his career out of NOT being brave: Rodger Ward.

The 500 was the race that counted, Indianapolis was the racetrack that the Offy roadster was bred for, and a dozen 500s in a row were won by roadsters. Roadsters, however, also won and set speed records and made history of one kind or another from Monza, Italy, to Mount Fuji, Japan, as well as Daytona International Speedway, where in 1959, the Simoniz 16 Watson won the fastest roadster race ever run, a sprint of 100 miles, at 170.261 miles per hour. The John Zink Leader Card 5 Watson won the 1958 Race of Two Worlds at Monza, Italy, at 166.733 miles per hour, which broke the closed-course record set in Germany by a factory Mercedes Benz W125 streamliner. The Bill Forbes Watson, which in 1962 was in the thick of the fight to exceed 150 miles per hour at Indy, in 1963 lapped a tire-testing bowl at 186.329 miles per hour, a world record that stood only a couple of weeks until the Sheraton-Thompson 2 Watson look-alike got up on the high walls at San Angelo, Texas, and A. J. Foyt cranked off the all-time unofficial speed record for roadsters of 200.4 miles per hour.

Roadsters such as the Bowes Seal Fast 14 Kurtis-Kraft and the John Zink 25 Watson occasionally showed up at championship dirt track meets like the Hoosier Hundred, and the Bowes Seal Fast 6 actually sat on the front row of the 1957 Phoenix dirt 100. As for road courses, anybody crazy enough to try and go racing around right-hand corners with a roadster—with 16 percent of the rolling weight preloaded to the left!—was asking for it; and, sure enough, during its 1965 Hoosier Grand Prix, the Indianapolis Raceway Park circuit really went to work on the Pope-Hall Watson, sending it flipping end for end.

Outside of Indy, Milwaukee's flat mile oval at the Wisconsin State Fair Park was the happiest hunting ground for dinosaurs. The Dunn Engineering, a mastodon Kurtis-Kraft, won Milwaukee's 250-miler of 1955, and the following year the same race was won by the Dean Van Lines 2, a Kuzma upright. By 1957 the race had been cut to 200 miles and was won by the Hopkins Chiropractic, an Epperly upright. Then in 1957 and 1958 the Wolcott Fuel Injection 8, the justly celebrated bent-engine Lesovsky/Porter, won a Milwaukee 100 and a Milwaukee 200; in 1959, another Lesovsky, the Racing Associates 3, won the Milwaukee 100.

Just like they did in the 500, though, Watsons led the way with ten Milwaukee scores in eight seasons, and that of the S-R Racing in 1960's summer 200 was surely the most spectacular of the ten. The Milwaukee mile that afternoon was thick with Watsons, including the Leader Card 1 on the pole. Scattered through the rest of the pack were the Dowgard, the Jim Robbins, the John Zink 28, the Agajanian, the Ken-Paul, and the Dean Van Lines.

Away they went. After leading for 59 miles, the Leader Card 1 fell back, spun out at 64 miles but kept going and fought back up to fourth, and then disappeared. This put the Dowgard into the lead, and at 175 miles a big scramble broke out between itself and a pair of low-belly laydowns, one a Kuzma and the other an Epperly, until one laydown stalled in the pits and the other on the backstraight and the Dowgard itself had a cockpit fire. And belatedly the S-R Racing came to life. Once as far behind as seventh, it moved to sixth, fifth, fourth, third, in and out of second, fell back to fourth, and finally went into the lead when the Dowgard arrived in the pits with its upholstery burning and its driver (Tony Bettenhausen) standing up in the seat with his left hand and wrist scorched. By the finish, the S-R Racing was a wreck. It had paid a stiff price for the victory: It had no

Milwaukee 200-miler pace lap in the summer of 1962. Rodger Ward in his Indy-winning Leader Card 3 Watson came off the pole position of the second row to win his sixth Wisconsin State Fair Park race in five seasons. He added a seventh in 1963 with the Kaiser Aluminum. *Armin Krueger*

Quin says "hi" to A. J. On the next-to-last corner of the 1961 Milwaukee 200, the Autolite 5 Epperly inexplicably smacks the John Zink 52 Watson. Watson driver Lloyd Ruby went on to win anyway; Epperly driver Jim Hurtubise lost control and took out himself and the pursuing Dean Van Lines 12 imitation Watson of Eddie Sachs. *Armin Krueger*

brakes, a gallon of fuel, the water pump was leaking, and steam was erupting from the radiator. The S-R Racing's driver was Len Sutton.

Nearly as big a win was the John Zink 8's in Milwaukee's 1956 100. Only 10 days prior it had won Indianapolis, but during Milwaukee practice the John Zink 8 lodged two dents in the back of slower cars and also spun out once. It qualified just eleventh fastest in a fast field of roadsters and dirt cars with only 100 laps to get to the front. But the John Zink 8 took just 9 laps to overtake five enemies and climb to sixth. On the 13th lap it was fifth, on the 15th, fourth, on the 23rd, third, on the 25th, second, and on the 57th it was leading and continued pulling away through the remaining 43. The John Zink 8's driver was Pat Flaherty.

Out of a dozen 100- and 200-mile races at Milwaukee between 1959 and 1964, Watsons only lost three. The winners were the Leader Card 5, the Leader Card 1, the Leader Card 2, the John Zink 52, the Bowes Seal Fast, the Leader Card 3, Kaiser Aluminum 1, and the Sheraton-Thompson 1. Rodger Ward and A. J. Watson were the driver and chief mechanic of the Leader Card 5, the Leader Card 1, the Leader Card 3, and the Kaiser Aluminum. Why they were so efficient there was perhaps a matter of job security: Bob Wilke, their employer, resided in Milwaukee.

Whatever, compared to other roadsters, Watsons had a lock on Milwaukee. At the Milwaukee 100 of 1960, the Watsons on hand were the Leader Card 1, S-R Racing, Dowgard, Dean Van Lines, Agajanian, and the Travelon Trailer, and after the 100 miles shook out they finished 1st, 3rd, 4th, 5th, 6th, 11th, and 20th. Watsons in the aforementioned Milwaukee 200 of 1960 were the S-R Racing, Jim Robbins, John Zink 28, Dowgard, Agajanian, Ken-Paul, Dean Van Lines, and Leader Card 1, and out of 26 roadsters and dirt trackers they finished 1st, 3rd, 14th, 17th, 18th, 20th, and 21st. One year afterward, in the 200 of 1961, the Watsons were the John Zink 52, S-R Racing, Bowes Seal Fast, Autolite 15, Dean Van Lines, and Leader Card 41, and they finished 1st, 2nd, 3rd, 5th, and 8th.

Unlike Indy, roadsters didn't devour their tires at Milwaukee or on the other miles; drivers could safely race through 100 and even 200 miles on the same set of Flintstones. Survival was scarcely guaranteed, however. The "Don't use the brakes!" deal of Indianapolis got ignored on Milwaukee's and Trenton's short and sharp corners, where only really hard braking could halt a ton of roadster.

But braking systems were inadequate and over a mile track race's final miles the pads were usually burned out with the pedal going to the floor. It was always the same on miles. No matter if one carried double discs on the rear, and no matter how frequently a chief mechanic changed calipers and linings, a roadster regularly surrendered its capacity to stop. There were no backups. Mounted to the fire wall was a single slave cylinder supplying the hydraulics, and if you blew out the piston it immediately pumped out all the fluid, which was what wrecked Len Sutton's Leader Card 7 at the 1962 Milwaukee 100. Losing its brakes while attempting to lap the Bell Lines Trucking, it hit the wall backwards hard enough to blow a hole in Len's right lung, collapse his lower back's second, third,

and fourth lumbar vertebrae, hospitalize him for a week, and knock him out of racing for almost two months. At that, Sutton was extremely fortunate that Fat Boy Ewing's 60-gallon tail fuel tank, which was squashed on impact, somehow deflated without leaking a proverbial drop of fuel. Had it done so and the Leader Card 7 caught fire, Len would have had to be saved by the same Milwaukee fire crew that couldn't rescue Smokey Elisian from his fully involved Travelon Trailer in 1959, or prevent Jim Hurtubise in his Tombstone Life from getting scarred to the third degree in 1964.

But perhaps the greatest menace that Kuzmas, Epperlys, Kurtis-Krafts, and Watsons faced at Milwaukee was the tricky traps set by Herb Porter. Indeed, what Herb's turbocharged Racing Associates 39 of a previous chapter almost did to all of Milwaukee's funny cars in 1966 was reminiscent of what Herb had done to adversary roadsters in earlier years.

In 1958, when the Zink Leader Card 5 arrived for Milwaukee's summer 200, it was practically roadster racing's best-known automobile. In less than four months it had set the fastest lap speed in the history of Indianapolis, been one of the three Watson instigators of the huge melee on the 500's opening lap, then had traveled to Italy and won all three heats of Monza's Race of Two Worlds. Herb was waiting for it with the Wolcott Fuel Injection 8. His then-driver was Rodger Ward, who won the Milwaukee race after forcing Jim Rathmann, driver of the John Zink 5, to blow it and spin out.

Herb's 8 was potent: "Now, on a mile track every Watson roadster pushed its front end, but my bent-engine eight ball just stuck to beat hell. It was superior. There was never any danger of spinning it out. All Ward had to do was go up on top, plant his fuckin' foot, get the car to take a set, then start coming off the corners 5 miles an hour faster than anybody else."

Watson was as curious about Herb's piece as anybody else. "A. J. Watson could get his roadsters running pretty good at Milwaukee," said Herb. "Matter of fact, a year or so later when Ward was driving for A. J. at Milwaukee and won the race, he told A. J. afterward, 'Well, it would've been a lot easier if I'd been driving Herb's bent-engine eight ball.' And a little later, Watson asked me how I'd designed my bent engine to get around a mile without pushing, and I said, 'A. J., one of these days maybe I'll tell you.' And you know what A. J. asked me after I did? 'Herb, you still got the blueprints and drawings?'"

In the Milwaukee 100 and 200 of 1962, Herb returned to upset the Watson status quo. It was during the time when Herb and Rocky Philipp were near the end of their co-chief mechanic partnership, and they brought with them a candy apple red dirt track champ car with a grunt stock block Chevrolet of 335 cubic inches whose edgy horsepower almost wasted all the Watsons and their antique Offys.

The "Little Red Rooster," as Herb named the stovebolt, got off to a smashed-up beginning along a desert stretch of Route 66 when Rocky fell asleep at the wheel hauling it back to the Midwest; everything crash-landed upside down, including Rocky, the tow rig, and the Little Red Rooster. But after a hasty repair job Herb's mighty rocker arm proved so alarming to all the Offenhausers that the U.S. Auto Club had to invent new rules to curb its explosive power. But not before the Little Red Rooster had managed to shame six famous Watsons in the Milwaukee 100 and help cripple a seventh one in the 200.

Starting ninth, Herb's big bow-tie went by the Bell Lines Trucking, the Leader Card 3, and the Leader Card 7. Then by the Jim Robbins. Then by the Agajanian Willard Battery. And at last around an Epperly laydown and then around the Bowes Seal Fast and into the lead at 32 miles. It would have continued to be a humiliating runaway if only the Little Red Rooster had had the Flintstones to keep it up; but after a blowout and long pit stop it fell behind and finished eighth. Merely to keep Herb's bellowing pushrod V-8 in sight, all Watson drivers had had to cheat the yellow cautions, so postmortem fines were dished out. The Bell Lines Trucking, the Jim

Robbins, the Bill Forbes, the Leader Card 3, the Agajanian Willard Battery, and the Gabriel Shocker all got docked prize money, as did the unfortunate Leader Card 7, even though it had taken Len Sutton backwards into the wall.

Later that August, Herb returned to raise more hell in the 200. Only this time the Little Red Rooster blew up and the huge oil puddle it laid down trapped a pack of Watsons, including the Bell Lines Trucking. Long, long after the accident concluded, not Herb's but a second dirt track Chevy—its driver playing blind man's bluff—came careening out of nowhere to meet the Bell Lines Trucking and clear off its oil tank, tweak its frame, and give it a wicked pulverizing.

*N*ear the 315-mile mark of the 1963 Indy 500, the John Zink Trackburner sprung an oil leak, lubricant hit its rear Flintstones, and it started getting sideways in its own spewing 50 weight. Driver Lloyd Ruby struggled and corrected and fought for control for the

Herk in trouble again! Hurtubise in his almost-to-150-miles-per-hour Travelon Trailer 56 of 1960 Indianapolis fame backs it too hot into Milwaukee's north turn. His dancing partner is Don Branson and the Bob Estes Phillips. *Armin Krueger*

length of a football field before at last smacking the outer wall. Afterward Lloyd accepted the glowing praise of Troy Ruttman, who'd been immediately behind him, for almost but not quite bringing the John Zink Trackburner back again. Ill-starred roadster master that he was, Troy well knew that a really canny driver could often have a roadster fly completely out of control at the Brickyard and then save it from crashing. Even when one took off in the wrong direction going for the wall, eight times out of ten it could be made to avoid the concrete just by the driver changing the path of the front wheels.

Still, when a whole pack of roadsters got into a wreck together they were such giant race cars that there wasn't room for avoidance. And, difficult as it was to avoid multidinosaur collisions in all the wide open spaces of Indy, it was impossible on a confining mile like Milwaukee's or Trenton's or Langhorne's, where in 1965 there was an especially bad and blazing pileup involving the Kemerly, a Lesovsky copy of a Watson, the Vita Fresh Orange Juice, a Kuzma copy of a Watson, and the Demler 99 Epperly.

At Milwaukee in the 1959 June 100, the Simoniz 16 Watson, unable to dodge the spinning Mirror-Glaze Kurtis-Kraft, jumped on top of it, piggyback. The driver of the Simoniz 16, Jim Rathmann, later collapsed from the delayed effects of a broken back. Two years later, in the summer Milwaukee 200 of 1961, the Dean Van Lines got torpedoed and taken out on the last corner by the Autolite 5 Epperly.

Various Trenton 100s, 150s, and 200s were won by the Leader Card 3, the Bowes Seal Fast, and the Sheraton-Thompson 1. Even so, Trenton could be a real graveyard for dinosaurs, and particularly Watsons, whose intramural crashfests seemed to occur every match.

In the spring of 1964, the Stearly Motor Freight 28 and the City of Victoria were dueling, and there was a big collision that took out both cars, plus a Leader Card funny car that had been leading the race. And just the previous 1963 summer that same often-hammered Stearly had center-punched the Federal Engineering, another Watson duplicate, which had begun traveling diagonally back across the track after first spanking the outside wall. The Stearly Motor Freight 28's driver, Eddie Sachs, got carried away to the infirmary with a concussion, fractured jaw, broken collarbone, loss of teeth, and a lacerated throat. All that battery occurred during morning practice. But in the afternoon 150-miler, three other Watsons and one Watson clone put on their own demo derby. The quartet was racing almost four abreast when the Kaiser Aluminum touched the Hook Lobster and got it out of shape, forcing the Leader Card 4

Lujie Lesovsky's and Herb Porter's Wolcott Fuel Injection Special, the "bent-engine eight ball," was in a class of its own at Milwaukee's 1958 200. Putting the move on Jim Rathmann and the Zink-Leader Card 5 Watson, one of A. J. Watson's favorite roadsters, Rodger Ward takes the lead he never lost. *Armin Krueger*

Bent-engine eight ball collaborators Lujie and Herb. *Lester Nehamkin, Ron Lesovsky collection*

and Leader Card 7 to get all tangled up and have to make spin-outs avoiding the spinning Hook Lobster.

One of the most destructive of all multi-Watson roadster accidents happened during the Trenton 200 of 1964. The Dayton Steel Wheel hit a puddle of oil and spun around, causing the Kemerly to make corrective moves, spin out anyway, then collect the Morcroft-Taylor, which next got hit by the Chapman. Raining sheets of alcohol from its ruptured fuel tank, the Chapman proceeded to circulate for one more lap anyway.

In the late summer of 1958, after the Bowes Seal Fast 14 Kurtis-Kraft flew endo out of Trenton, broke in half on impact, and killed Jimmy Reece, the state of New Jersey declared itself unsatisfied with prevailing safety provisions and mandated that all dinosaurs come equipped with cockpit rollover bars. The U.S. Auto Club made them mandatory everywhere, and in the 1964 Trenton 100 a rollover bar was what saved the Dayton Steel Wheel Watson from utter destruction.

The Bell Lines Trucking Watson, outside, feels the heat and caves in to the pressure of another Porter concoction, Herb's raging Chevy stock-block, the Little Red Rooster. *Armin Krueger*

The Dayton Steel Wheel, formerly the Bell Lines Trucking, was regularly on the receiving end of some awfully bad action. New in 1962, it had spun to a stop in its own radiator coolant at Indy and also received a crashing at Milwaukee. Though straightened once, its still-deformed frame had caused it to miss the 1963 500. And then down the Trenton back straightway in 1964 it succeeded in sparking along on its top after getting turned turtle and spilled from behind by the Dean Van Lines.

If it hadn't been for the Dayton Steel Wheel's protective roll hoop keeping some of the racetrack away, Trenton might well have scrapped off even more roadster pieces and done worse damage to the Dayton than it did. As it was, the Watson looked like it had gotten dropped off a building. Only an ardent crash-hound and roadster repairman extraordinaire like Buster Warke, the Dayton's chief, could possibly have effected repairs quickly enough to be at Indianapolis only two weeks later for the opening of 500 practice.

Unable to avoid the chaos caused by the 1961 Milwaukee collision of the Zink 52 and Autolite 5, the Dean Van Lines ran out of room and met the wall. Dean chief mechanic Clint Brawner, left, smolders over it. *Armin Krueger*

Following pages: The first big season for Rodger Ward, A. J. Watson, and Leader Card was 1959. Rodger won the Indy 500, the Milwaukee 200, here, in the Leader Card 5 (outside), plus a pair of dirt track 100s and the seasonal national championship. Rodger and A. J. in subsequent campaigns reinforced the Leader Card lock on Milwaukee by adding power steering. Rodger: "A Watson roadster with power steering on that smooth Milwaukee race track . . . we just blew 'em all off." *Armin Krueger*

Throwing himself on the mercy of fellow Watson chiefs, Buster got Johnnie Pouelsen to loan him a spare front axle off the Agajanian Bowes Seal Fast; and Barney Wimmer helped out with a drag link, torsion bars, and other components off the Sarkes-Tarzian. Barely repaired in time, and still not completely painted, the patchwork Dayton Steel Wheel broke 150 miles per hour and was runner-up among second-day Indy qualifiers.

Regrettably for Buster Warke, though, all this heroic effort was fated to turn into another of those wonderful "Nothing's perfect!"

chief mechanic experiences. During the 500, the Dayton Steel Wheel came so close to the holocaust on the second lap that its new paint job got scorched. And then it couldn't even make it to the half distance mark before running over some debris and going twirling out of the 500.

During the Dayton Steel Wheel's berserk and upside-down ride across the Trenton back-straight, its driver, Troy Ruttman, was fortunate to be properly restrained by seatbelts and harnesses and

In company with a backwards dirt car, the Bob Estes Phillips does the Trenton twist. Making it through on the bottom is the John Zink 52. *Bruce Craig*

After sitting on pole position with a track record and finishing third in the 1959 Indy 500, then winning Milwaukee's June 100-miler, the sexy pink Racing Associates 3 Lesovsky lowbelly laydown was the early leader of Milwaukee's August 200-miler. But it faded. The following May at Indy It broke down while making a late bid for the lead. And then in the 1960 Milwaukee 100 it broke again. Sad. The roadster, developed with the assistance of safety design consultant Norm Benedict, was ahead of its time and deserved a better fate. *Armin Krueger*

During Trenton's 150-miler of 1963, Don Branson and the Leader Card 4 first had to get backwards when confronting the spinning Hook Lobster 43; then, they were nearly run over by the onrushing Konstant Hot 14 and Dean Van Lines 10. *Bruce Craig*

therefore did not get physically harmed at all. But because Troy was a 6-foot-3, 230-pound hulk and all of him seldom fit inside a road-ster cockpit, the adventure allowed the Trenton asphalt to abrade two layers of his crash helmet.

Troy was oversized in all ways, and his preternatural skills intimidated one and all. The brightest member of the flashy cast of West Coast rodders who were hitting the Brickyard in the late for-ties, Troy was the first L.A. boy to win the 500, aged a whole 22. Yet long before becoming the 500's youngest champion, Ruttman, who started racing at 16, had had a career full of doing impossible deeds everywhere from Langhorne to the old Mexican Road Race to the notorious Salem Speedway. In the words of one of his chief mechanics, "Troy could drive anything he wanted to, and he would make things work that nobody else would try." But following his

1952 Indy win, Troy had broken his arm in a sprint car, grown fat and out of shape while convalescing, and then had gotten clob-bered blindside by standard race driver sin goodies such as liquor and wild women.

Almost any owner of an Offy roadster might have given any-thing to have Ruttman race for him at Indy or anywhere, except that Troy wouldn't lay off the booze or behave himself. Time after time his bad habits led to sanctioning bodies suspending him. Consequently, Troy got a well-deserved reputation for being a flaky and dissolute prima donna, too undependable for most car owners to invest in him.

What a loss for roadster racing! Throughout the era, Troy was only allowed to race second-rate or worse equipment. At Indy in 1956, Jack Zink and A. J. Watson gave him the John Zink 53, a

year-old Kurtis-Kraft, and made Pat Flaherty the gift of their new John Zink 8 Watson. But Troy intuitively recognized the very first Watson for the great race car it was, and subsequently became one of the coaches who helped teach Flaherty to race without using brakes. How he did it was vintage Troy· After wiring off the brake pedal of the John Zink 8, he bet Pat a sawbuck that he, Troy, could lap 3 miles per hour faster brakeless than Pat could using brakes. Troy won the bet, and Pat soon had the John Zink 8 zooming brakeless.

The following year, 1957, with Flaherty still recovering from dirt track wounds, Troy got to race Watson's new John Zink 52. He found it even more race car than the John Zink 8. Unhappily, prior to the 500 he fell back on his prima donna ways by refusing to take hardly any practice laps. Still, after he qualified on the front row, then shot into an ever-widening lead, all seemed OK again with

Troy. But after the John Zink 52 next fell out of the show with a mysterious case of overheating in only 24 minutes, there were two conflicting explanations of what had really happened. One account had it that the Zink 52 had had a thermostat installed at the last moment, and its Offenhauser hadn't liked it. The other suggested version was that throughout the month the radiator had had an air pocket, a condition that went unremedied only because Troy had neglected to take adequate practice laps.

In 1960 he had the worn and weathered John Zink 28 in the lead and in orbit when he had to quit because the least expensive component in the Watson mix, its gearshift lever, snapped off in his hand. In 1961, again leading or near the lead and attempting to make an extra-fast pit stop with the same car, Troy cooked the clutch.

Next to Rodger Ward, Ruttman probably raced in more different Watsons and Watson clones than anybody else, including—in a dazzling pair of Trentons in 1962 and 1963—the Stearly Motor Freight 28. This was right at a time when a lot of people were doubting that the former child wonder had any excellent racing left in him, and Troy felt obliged to demonstrate that he did. In the Trenton 100 of 1963 he qualified a poor 16th and then caught all the leaders inside of 70 miles. But he'd gone through the binders and had to race without brakes over the last 30 laps. Still going flat out and somehow hanging onto control, Troy at last lost it with less than a lap to go. Going into the third corner railing broadside, the Stearly Motor Freight 28 hit so hard that all four wheels lifted a yard off the track. Following this it coasted around for the remainder of the lap to still come in fifth. To finally get it stopped, Troy had had to bludgeon it against the pit wall.

He and the Stearly had made an even stronger showing in the Trenton 200 the previous winter. This time they were in it from the start, and it was between them and Rodger Ward in the Leader Card 3, the duo that had just won Indianapolis. Rodger was on the pole but Troy overcame him for 6 miles until Rodger recovered and repassed high around the second corner. Troy regained and lost the position at 11 miles, then did the same thing at 19. Running single file with Rodger through heavy traffic for the next 60 miles, Troy was tenacious and went into first place again at 88 miles. Five miles later Rodger swept back into first again, then at 133 miles tangled with a lapped car, and the Leader Card 3 spun out and fell two laps behind. Meanwhile Troy and the Stearly Motor Freight led at 140 miles, 150 miles, 160 miles—before at last going down and out with a slipping clutch at 173.

Rodger had hustled back with the Leader Card 3 to finish fifth. But the 200's winner was Don Branson, exceeding all the roadsters in his old-fashioned Leader Card champ dirt car. At Trenton, though, that wasn't considered an upset. Offy roadsters had their aerodynamic advantages over the taller dirt car, and their offset chassis made them physically easier to turn left. But even with its air jacks and other 500-mile bric-a-brac removed, a roadster was still a couple of hundred pounds heavier than a dirt car. In 1962, Milwaukee had watched Herb Porter's Little Red Rooster almost put it over on all the dinosaurs, and in 1955 and 1958 the Peter Schmidt 44 and the Central Excavating 81—a glorious pair of Kuzma dirt trackers—had done the same deed. So at Trenton, too, the fiercest enemy a roadster might have was a dirt car that had an inspired chauffeur like Branson straddling its driveshaft.

Or before him, Eddie Sachs.

Recalling a roadster race at Trenton that he lost and "that absolutely blew my mind," Rodger Ward discussed 1960's fall 100 when he was driving the former Leader Card 5: "I started quite aways back, but once they dropped the green flag I was off and working my way through traffic. One of the first guys I passed—no problem—was Sachs in his dirt car. And in spite of being cautious and saving the brakes so I'd have some at the end, I was already in the lead by 70 miles. At that point I figured it's all over—I'm gone.

"But suddenly A. J. Watson is giving me a board that somebody is eight seconds behind, then five. So I start driving my brains out, but next thing, Watson is clear out on the racetrack clapping his hands and signaling that I'm being CAUGHT. And before I can even imagine who's back there, this goddamn Eddie Sachs in his dirt car just drives around the outside of me and DISAPPEARS. And earlier I just passed him without giving him a thought. Miracles do happen!"

To Sachs they certainly did, and usually at Trenton, including the time he flew out of the place and survived without a scratch. In the Trenton 100s of 1959 and 1960 Eddie beat all the roadsters with a dirt track Meskowski, then did it twice more in 1961 with his Dean Van Lines Kuzma. In one of them, his hard-running Offy dropped an exhaust valve with 55 miles to go, smoke began pouring out, and somehow Eddie summoned the wherewithal to race on to victory turning faster lap times on three cylinders than he had with four.

No other mile track defeat that all the roadsters ever suffered was more humiliating.

Symbolic of the way careening roadsters were unable to avoid one another on the tight confines of mile tracks was this 1959 Milwaukee piggyback job involving the Simoniz 16 Watson and Chapman 43 Kurtis-Kraft. The melee gave Simoniz 16 pilot Jim Rathmann a broken back. *Armin Krueger*

Previous pages: The virtuoso who never got his due: Troy Ruttman *Bob Tronolone*

Chapter 7

THE BIGGEST BATTLE

The Ken-Paul versus the Leader Card 1

Chasing down roadster memories, on June 24, 1994, a hot and muggy afternoon in Indianapolis, I was paying a visit to the Hall of Fame Museum to examine the Ken-Paul, the Watson roadster that had fought and beaten another Watson, the Leader Card 1, to win the longest sustained battle of the roadster age. But I was beginning to feel bad even before I went inside. NASCAR stock cars from the Winston Cup were out on the track doing testing for their inaugural Brickyard 400 later that summer, and just the thought of taxi cabs competing at the Speedway made me think about how far Indianapolis has fallen since the dinosaurs.

But I went in anyway, and before checking out the Ken-Paul I looked with admiration at the other Watsons on display, all of them 500 winners, the Agajanian Willard Battery, the Leader Card 3, and the Sheraton-Thompson 1. None of them, to my eyes, could compare with the metallic blue Ken-Paul. No less than A. J. Watson had called it the best one that 421 West Palmer turned out in 1960, and all the meticulous prepping and mother-henning that Chickie Hirashima brought to the Ken-Paul is part of roadster lore. The oil well and Stetson logo of Kenny Rich and Paul Lacey, the car's owners, looked as fine as ever, and Jim Rathmann was still identified as the Ken-Paul's driver. But Smokey Yunick's name as chief mechanic had been erased, and I knew why. I was also glad that no rabid Offy roadster historians or Watson collectors were there with me, because I knew they'd have picked apart the restored Ken-Paul as sham from one end to the other: Its hood and much of its coachwork actually belongs on the Leader Card 1, as does its starter shaft, shock absorber covers, and other integral pieces. And all of the original running gear, suspension components, and torsion

bars, plus Fat Boy Ewing fuel tanks and the wonderful Halibrand hubs and hex cap bolts that Chickie so fanatically drilled out just to save a few ounces—the Ken-Paul was the lightest Watson in the 500—were nowhere to be seen.

Not caring to be distracted by any of that for the moment, I continued looking at the Ken-Paul and remembering the 1960 Indianapolis 500. And then I recalled that Jim Rathmann in the Ken-Paul and Rodger Ward in the Leader Card 1 hadn't been the only adversaries that timeless day, and that two of my chief mechanic heroes, Rocky Philipp and Herb Porter, had had a roadster of their own that was running really fast—faster than either the Ken-Paul or the Leader Card 1. So, outside the museum again, I decided to walk over to Gasoline Alley and see if Herb was there.

Gasoline Alley caught "cement fever" in the mid-eighties when its old and combustible wooden sheds got torn down, and the whole homey garage area got turned concrete gray with as much atmosphere as San Quentin penitentiary. None of its nineties occupants looked like people you could discuss Offy roadsters with, except for Herb, who was at home as ever inside his stall at the intersection across from the Goodyear compound. He greeted me with the familiar stern Porter glare, but didn't tell me to get out and even consented to answer a few questions.

From outside came the noise of taxicabs practicing, and we both expressed dissatisfaction about stock cars being let loose on Indianapolis. "I appreciate the NASCAR guys," Herb allowed, "and I know they got a lot of good people. And they do a lot of good work. But if they got fenders and headlights on 'em, they ain't race cars to Herb."

I concurred wholeheartedly, and for a moment hoped we'd next get to cut to a no-holds-barred discussion of one of my great

Rathmann leads Ward! By official count, Jim and Rodger did this half a dozen times across the starting strip, each one robbing the other of his lap prize money, but made four times as many lead swaps out on the Speedway. With three laps to go, they remained in a dead heat.
Indy 500 Photos

Smokey Yunick. NASCAR's most celebrated stock car wrench had a thing about being toasted an Indy 500-winning chief mechanic and thought the 1960 race had made him one. *Indy 500 Photos*

irritations—namely, how it happened that all the roadsters of this book somehow succeeded in living up to their dinosaur nickname and disappearing. Literally! The era happened so quickly, 1952 to 1964, then phoot! everything got replaced by those nowhere funny cars.

What really made the Offy roadsters die such unnatural deaths?

My own ideas are that the masterminds running the Brickyard never quite realized or appreciated what they had when Indianapolis was a satellite of Los Angeles and was a fun, silly place filled with roadsters and roadster people. Don't believe what you've been told or read, it's all jive, the miserable Ford-powered Lotuses and the other wiggle cars of the "rear-engine revolution" with their uncontrollable and empty technology and ridiculously high speeds and absence of wheel-to-wheel racing—the little bastards aren't that wonderful. It was the muscular and unsophisticated dinosaurs with their good old Meyer-Drake Offenhausers, their free-spirit car owners, their buddy-buddy chief mechanics, and their swaggering drivers, who were the perfect expression of red-blooded, made-in-America racing.

But the brains operating Indy didn't see it that way, and so they became the ones who did it to us; they turned over custodianship of the 500 to Colin Chapman and all those other jolly blokes whose mission wasn't to assimilate the Offy roadster culture but to obliterate it. And then make it Brit.

And there's something else that needs to be added. What sapped the roadster spirit at Indy wasn't just the Hoosier Clem mentality of the Indianapolis Motor Speedway; or the stupidity and myopia of the disgraced U.S. Auto Club; or all those Offy roadster owners, builders, mechanics, and drivers who either became rah-rah cheerleaders for the funny cars or else indifferently went along with them without a fight; or even the scheming Brits. Rather, it was the corrosive influence of the Big Money, which began with the mega-bucks of the Ford Motor Company, and was immediately followed by the devious and greedy rubber wars fought by Firestone and Goodyear.

"The sickness of the world," groaned an old boxing manager, deploring what mega-dollars did to professional pugilism. And before Indianapolis crashed and burned into the second-rate spectacle it has become, the long green was doing the same thing to the 500, which every May took on the soulless atmosphere of corporate big business with upscale modern teams attempting to outspend the Pentagon. Trying to keep up, famous roadster squads like Leader Card got squashed, and the only way that Ralph Wilke, the late Bob's son, could afford to continue racing in the eighties and nineties was to sell the driving compartment to wealthy but talentless buy-a-rides. I once talked briefly to one of Leader Card's pseudo-race driver atrocities whom A. J. Watson had to put up with in his last chief mechanic years—there's no point in revealing the joker's name—and discovered that he was a wine and sporty car snob with a bachelor of science degree in marketing and was president of his own "Motorsports Promotion" outfit promoting himself. He had no competition record to speak of. He also had no historical perspective

whatever—he assumed Brit rear-engines had always won the 500. He had no idea there'd been such a thing as a Watson roadster.

I had lots of fun imagining this greenhorn surrounded by a ton of vibrating roadster, getting hammered by noise and stress for 500 miles, having to take corners without using the brakes, and having all the raging radiant heat off the Offenhauser blowing back through the uncovered cockpit fire wall, cooking his butt. And I thought with malicious pleasure of him inhaling some of the oil and tire junk that was getting plastered all over his yuppie mug. . . .

The roadster decline and fall was sweeping and pervasive. The number of roadsters in the 500 declined in 1966 to one, and by 1967 there were none. Everything about the era was systematically erased and seeing all of it vanish made it a terrible time to live through. As a malcontent and unreformed dinosaur man, I still get slightly hysterical about it. Maybe more than slightly, Herb came to notice.

Herb disagreed totally. Herb thought I was crazy. "Never cared for the past," he announced dismissively. "Only thing that interests Herb is the racing right now." As a matter of fact, as we hit the millennium Herb was still staying busy in his 80s hopping up Aurora Olds engines for the Indianapolis Racing League!

Tired of being a sourpuss, I got back to the real purpose of my visit.

"What about that Lujie car you and Rocky Philipp had in the 1960 500?" I prompted, and Herb's memory was off like a shot, maybe because that particular vehicle, the Adams Quarter-Horse, a year-old Lesovsky, really had been remarkable, and perhaps had even deserved to win the 500 more than the Ken-Paul. It was the same lowbelly laydown, painted naughty pink, which had sat on the pole in 1959, then finished third after Herb and Rocky and Lujie had had a violent argument on the pit road about a damaged weight jacker.

"It was a copy of my old bent-engine Walcott eight ball," Herb began. "A real fine race car. Johnny Thomson was driving it. Only, the car was puzzling John. 'Herb, what am I doing wrong?' he'd asked. So we'd sat down in a restaurant and over steaks and a couple three drinks I got out a napkin to draw on and told him the theory behind the car and what he needed to do to drive it. And me and Rocky adjusted the chassis and a couple of days later John said to me, 'Goddamn, Herb, you're right. She works just like you told me.'

"Then in the 500 he was eight seconds behind Rathmann and Ward and their Watsons and gaining to beat hell with 25 miles left. He'd already blown off Ward once, down in the first corner, and after the race Rodger said, 'I knew what was going to happen when he caught us. He'd just drive around on the outside and go on.' And John did have Indy fuckin' WON that year. Until he dropped a valve. And that's where I got this."

Herb pointed at a white mark on his wrist.

"John came into the pits with the engine running rough, and just then the head of an exhaust valve came flying off and hit me. Rocky was on the other side of the car yelling, 'We're on three cylinders!' And I yelled back, 'Fuck yes we are, there's a head off a valve, look here.'"

Knowing that Rodger Ward, Rocky Philipp, and the late Johnny Thomson all might have had quibbles with Herb's version of the 1960 500, it still would have been churlish of me to do anything but thank Herb for all his information and time, and I most sincerely did.

Outside of Gasoline Alley again, I went by the Speedway Motel and stopped at the bar, hoping that 1960's big Ken-Paul victory party might still be in hot progress. Then I cruised the Speedway Motel's swimming pool. Nobody was in the water, not even Bunkie Hunt, who all those decades before had been one of many ultrarich Texans who'd taken a dunking with their clothes on. And then just to make myself feel really poorly, I swung by the bunker on 16th Street that used to be the White Front. It looked semideserted. "Lots of guys would roll over in their graves knowing that for several years the White Front ended up turning into a gay bar," Duke Cook, another roadster diehard, had warned me. "Now it's a go-go titty bar."

Bad, bad deal. Instead of getting a buzz from overdosing on all the nostalgia, I was reeling from disappointment instead. Yet how could it have been otherwise? Everything seemed tainted.

The Leader Card 1 ran second to the Ken-Paul in 1960's red-hot 500 and the next week won the Milwaukee 100. In 1964, called the Chapman 23, it went to Trenton and grappled past a dozen roadsters and funny cars in just 56 miles, got all tangled up in a typical multidinosaur mile track wreck, then continued circulating anyway. In 1968, at Hanford, California, it was the last Watson able to qualify and start in a championship race. Named the Vince Conze Special, its horsepower was that of a dinky 220 cubic inch Offenhauser borrowed from a Pikes Peak hill climb rig. *Indy 500 Photos*

Taxicabs were circling the Brickyard, the Speedway Motel was filled with tourists in souvenir NASCAR shirts, and what the Hall of Fame purported to be the winning Ken-Paul was really a hodgepodge that was mostly the Leader Card 1. Thirty-four Memorial Days prior, the Ken-Paul and the Leader Card 1 had engaged in Indy's epic 500. And in one of the 500's most bitter aftermaths, the winning driver Jim Rathmann and his lifelong racing friend Smokey Yunick had become nonspeaking enemies, with Smokey still raging after all this time that he'd taken a royal screwing from Jim and had been deprived of the credit for being 1960's champion chief mechanic.

Smokey remembered their falling out. "I liked Rathmann at first, you know. And then after he jerked me around and double-crossed me and lied like a sonuvabitch it finally dawned on me what a no-good bastard he was. And I've told him, 'Rathmann, if I see you first, I'm going to cross the street. And if you see me first, you'd better be the one who crosses the street.'"

Jim sees it another way. "Smokey was never the chief mechanic. He knows better than that. I don't give a damn, there's no money out of my pocket either way. But in fact Smokey doesn't like me because of that. Because I wouldn't lie for him. He was crew chief on race day only. I've told Smokey that to his face."

Ward and Rathmann already had firsthand knowledge of each other's dinosaur repertory. Here at Milwaukee in 1957, three years before their big showdown at the Speedway, they go at it, Rodger in his bent-engine eight ball Lesovsky, Jim in an Epperly. *Armin Krueger*

White Flintstone cord flashing on its right rear, the winning Ken-Paul comes rolling home to Gasoline Alley after 500 winning miles at a Brickyard-record 139 miles per hour. *Indy 500 Photos*

The 1960 500 was the peak of the Watson roadster. All the first two rows were Watsons or Watson knockoffs, with the Dean Van Lines and Eddie Sachs on the pole, the Ken-Paul and Rathmann in the middle, and the Leader Card 1 and Rodger Ward on the outside. The second row was all Watson, too, with the Jim Robbins, the S-R Racing, and the John Zink 28 of Troy Ruttman. Mixed through the rest of the field were the Agajanian, the Leader Card 66, the Dowgard, and the 149,030-mile-per-hour Travelon Trailer of Jim Hurtubise.

Sachs, Rathmann, Ward, and Ruttman all mixed it up from the beginning. Chopping down hard on Rathmann and Sachs at the first corner, Rodger led the opening lap. Then Eddie led, then Troy led, then Jim, then Rodger, then Eddie, then Troy, then Eddie, then Jim, then Eddie, then Jim, and then Johnny Thomson and the Adams-Quarter Horse up from 17th. The first refueling and tire stops were made, and Rodger lost 40 seconds stalling his engine. "After that," Rodger told me in an interview, "I was driving the wheels off the damn thing to catch up again. And then Rathmann and I—you may recall—had one hellacious race."

Rodger understates. The battle between those two perfectly matched 1960 Watsons had the whole Speedway spellbound. Rathmann and Ward had a slew of official lead changes at the start and finish strip, but out on the track made possibly four times that many. Together making their last fuel and rubber stops at 390 miles, the Ken-Paul and the Leader Card 1 raced each other in and out of the pits for the last time. Having lined up for the 500 side-by-side some 493 insane miles earlier, the Ken-Paul and the Leader Card 1 bombed across the front straightaway still dead-heated with three laps to go.

By then both Jim and Rodger, struggling for any advantage, were monkeying around with their cockpit weight jackers. The "weight jacker" of a Watson was a good news/bad news device. Consisting of a simple ratchet attached to two bolts to move the preloaded torsion bars and modify the static weight distribution, the good news was that a dinosaur driver using his weight jacker wisely could make a Watson lap faster; the bad news was, the faster it lapped, the quicker it cooked its tires. Canvas on the right front Flintstone of Rodger's Leader Card 1 started showing at the same time that it did on the right rear of Jim's Ken-Paul, but Rodger didn't realize that what was happening to him, was also happening to Jim. Always the most self-preservation minded of all dinosaur drivers, Rodger instead cooled his pace and let the Ken-Paul go. Having already clocked the 500's fastest lap speed, Jim sped on to win by 13 seconds at a record average. In Victory Lane the Ken-Paul's right

rear was showing cord; it should have blown out, but hadn't. The first thing Jim asked was, "What happened to Ward?"

The greatest 500 of the roadster days and I was at home in L.A. and not present to see it! One way to compensate for not being back at Indy on Memorial Day used to be to drive up to Santa Barbara for the weekend road races at the Goleta airport. Memorial Day 1960 fell on a Monday, and a bunch of us were returning from Santa Barbara with the car radio on listening to the 500. All the vibes were wrong. My companions were sporty car people, and nobody in the car was much of a fan of Indianapolis but me. I never cared for the broadcasting style of the self-proclaimed "Voice of the 500," Sid Collins. And the 500 had barely gotten underway when all of us in the car heard the emergency news flash saying that there had been two deaths and 40 injuries from the collapse of one of those tall and Jerry-built spectator scaffolds on the Speedway infield. But gradually what I'd thought was the triple whammy of being with the wrong company, listening to the wrong announcer, and having the 500 get off to the wrong beginning, changed. All of us in the car were steadily drawn into the high drama of the battling Ken-Paul and Leader Card 1. By the closing 100 miles, everybody realized that something was really going on. And by the battle's end, just about the time that Jim Rathmann was in Victory Circle contemplating his Ken-Paul's bald right rear Flintstone, our car was parked on a stretch of seacoast between Ventura and Oxnard. The driver had to stop so that all of us could collectively and literally grab our breaths again.

Ever since then, the 1960 500 has stayed on my mind, and through the decades I've tried to learn everything about it I can, including collecting anecdotes from most of the belligerents involved who are still alive—doing it for fun, you understand, never imagining that one day I'd get to put it all in a book. Oddly enough, it wasn't until fairly recently that I finally got to talk to Jim Rathmann and Rodger Ward themselves.

On a magazine assignment to write a Jim Rathmann profile, I'd gone to Melbourne, Florida, which is Jim's longtime home and the place he ran a big automotive dealership just down the beach from the NASA Space Program at Cape Canaveral. He once hobnobbed with the original seven astronauts. We talked racing at the dealership, and at his expensive home on the water and at his country club, where he handed me a business card:

Jim Rathmann,
CEO, Jim Rathmann Cadillac

I still have the card and regard it as an almost-one-of-a-kind souvenir. Next to Parnelli Jones, Jim is the only dinosaur driver I ever met who retired to become a big-shot millionaire CEO. Probably it was preordained. No matter how talented a race car driver Jim always was, he was equally talented at discovering ways to make the large moola, beginning very early in Chicago where he'd

Would you buy a used dinosaur from this man? A formidable race driver in his own right, Rodger Ward additionally liked to dissemble, get inside the brains of his opponents, and use the big con. Anything to get an extra advantage. "I am not nearly as brave as I once was on the race track," Rodger fibbed, actually expecting the younger foes he trimmed all the time to believe him. *Indy 500 Photos*

been the pet of Andy Granatelli and one of the kid stars of the hell-on-wheels Hurricane hot rods. Every five nights Jim was winning close to $10,000 and wondering how to spend it. Not quite 21, Jim was already tooling around the Windy City in a new Caddy.

Even when he started racing in the 500, Indianapolis wasn't enough for him. On the side Jim was operating a successful speed shop in Miami, was earning a small fortune shipping used De Soto engines to South America, was manufacturing and marketing his own brand of go-kart, and working in semisecret for General Motors, presiding over Chevrolet's stock car racing program. Finally getting out of race driving in 1964, he continued parlaying enterprises. Being Jim Rathmann Cadillac's CEO was hardly his only title. At the time we spoke, Jim had additionally passed time as a cable TV entrepreneur and gulf coast real estate tycoon. For a while he'd even gotten caught up in the treasure-hunting business: With a cartel of investment partners, he'd gone searching for lost Spanish galleons along Florida's shallow east coast.

While Jim talked and I listened, I remembered something Rodger Ward once said about him: "Jim Rathmann was one of those race drivers that when he could see you would automatically find an extra couple of miles an hour."

Meaning, naturally, that in the tradition of other gunners of the Offy roadster such as his older brother, Dick, of "braver than Dick Rathmann" notoriety, Jim was another attack-on-sight driver. Other than their hereditary baldness, though, it was hard imagining that the Rathmanns were of the same family. Strapping on a roadster automatically made Dick upright and ferociously aggressive. But Jim, unless he had the stimulus of other race cars to attack, might became so indifferent and sluggish it was a wonder that he'd never fallen asleep at the wheel.

Another thing was, he knew how to run the rules and work the Indy regulations to his personal advantage. A smart cookie. There were always a few scoundrels in roadster 500s who tried violating the yellow caution flags and stealing as much track as possible without getting caught, and Jim could be such a scoundrel. Sometimes his behavior could be outrageous. In 1959, he was lead-footing his Simoniz 16 through one of the yellow slow-downs and so aggressively eroding the lead of Ward in the Leader Card 5, that A. J. Watson in the pits had to get Jim off Rodger's back by blackboarding the message *CHEATER RATHMANN* to provoke Rodger into illegally speeding up himself.

Jim Rathmann, then, was cool, calculating, opportunistic, mercenary, and brazen—not only did he and the Ken-Paul win the defining roadster battle, but he and the Simoniz 16 established the world speed record winning at Daytona, and he and the Zink-Leader Card 5 captured Monza's ultrafast Race of Two Worlds. But what I think was fascinating and maybe most frightening about Jim was that at certain dangerous moments he possessed a risk-everything streak; when he wanted to he could be just as self-destructive a gambler as Smokey Elisian. And on the electrifying 493rd mile of the 1960 500 he'd literally put his life on the line wagering he could lead to the finish on a threadbare Flintstone. And won.

During my interview with him, one of the last questions I put to Jim concerned what he might have done had Rodger Ward not withdrawn from the battle—if on the final corner the Ken-Paul and the Leader Card 1 were still barreling wheel-to-wheel. I thought he'd say something about deploying some old dirty trick he'd learned from Hurricane hot rods, but Jim's answer surprised me. "I'd have pulled an 'Andy Linden at Bonelli Stadium,'" he replied.

Andy Linden was the tattooed navy boxer and L.A. hot-rod alumnus and one-time Herb Porter driver who later crash-landed on his head in an Offy midget and had to be put in an asylum. He spent a third of his life in a wheelchair. But years and years earlier, racing hot rods against Andy in a trophy dash at Bonelli Stadium, Jim with the faster rod had lost the dash after Andy, in front of him, pulled some short-braking shenanigans. So I interpreted Jim to mean that in the 1960 500 he would have employed such tactics on Ward.

*B*ut it's hard to imagine that they would have worked. Not against Rodger, at least, who had more seat time in various Watsons than anybody else, who could haul ass in one with a full load of fuel faster than anyone else, and who was savvy about never racing without holding something in reserve.

When Rodger and I met to talk about the 1960 500 it was back in California at a restaurant in Ontario close to where the old Motor Speedway had stood. This was in the summer of 1994, and my previous visit to the Hall of Fame Museum had occurred just a couple of months earlier. Rodger looked in as great shape as ever, and the Ward syntax and photographic memory were cooking. He recalled everything, including his own first corner chop job of Jim and Eddie Sachs that put him into the lead. And then Rodger recalled how, after checking out those of Jim, Eddie, and Troy Ruttman, he verified to his satisfaction that his Leader Card 1 was indeed the 500's fastest Watson.

"Maybe Mr. Rathmann won't forgive me for saying it now," Rodger said, "but I had him covered. Or I thought I did until I killed my engine on that first pit stop.

"Leader Card had a new man on the pit crew that year, and it was Art Lamey, who for years had done my stock cars and who'd wanted to work at Indianapolis. And I'd wanted him to work at Indianapolis. So A. J. Watson put him on the crew, changing the right front. The rest of the crew was always superb, I had no concern with any of them, and as I was watching Art change the right front, he was finished before everybody else. And that made me so confident right there that I was already rehearsing what I was going to say when I arrived in Victory Circle. So when Watson hit me on the hat to go, I put the car in gear, released the clutch, and forgot to step on the gas and the engine died.

"I sat there for another 40 seconds while they restarted it. And of course when I got out of the pits, instead of leading again I was half a lap behind. So I jacked in a couple of turns of weight and took off after 'em, driving the wheels off the thing. And in a relatively

Per Rodger, A. J. Watson's hottest roadster-building winter was 1959–1960, when the Head turned out his seventh, eighth, ninth, and tenth dinosaurs, including the co-belligerents of the bellwether 1960 500, Rodger's Leader Card 1 and Jim Rathmann's Ken-Paul. They seemed sleeker and nicer-looking than Watsons of later vintage. More important, they appeared to be the best balanced—as Rodger commented, a driver could do things with one of them that he couldn't do with other roadsters. *Indy 500 Photos*

Above and opposite: Looking to duplicate the big 500 of 1960, Smokey Yunick and Jim Rathmann did two more Indys together in 1961 (30th) and 1962 (9th). Before breaking down, they were fast enough to win again in '61, but pathetic in '62. *Indy 500 Photos*

Watson and Ward, two of Leader Card's "three Ws." The Head on Ward: "Rodger was the easiest driver I ever had work for me. He used to come in and ask how fast he was going. And I'd say he was half a second off. 'Well,' he'd say, 'I guess I have to get with it.' He never gave excuses." *Indy 500 photos*

short period of time I was back fighting Rathmann for the lead of the race, and figuring I had it made all over again. Only I wasn't smart enough to remember that with extra chassis weight tires wore out faster, and to jack the weight out after I'd caught Rathmann.

"Faugh! Rathmann and I made our third and last stops and came out of the pits together, and I wasn't thinking that tires were going to be that serious of a problem—normally the Speedway gets a little oily at the end, and as you ran slower the tires lasted longer. So I decided it was time to put some distance between myself and Rathmann and ran hard for seven or eight laps. But then I looked at my right front and, oh God, that new tire was already showing excessive wear. And I still hadn't been able to put any significant amount of distance between Rathmann and myself.

"The only thing I could do was let Rathmann pass me and lead the race and then hope that he would slow down. When I say LET him past, I'm sure that he wouldn't agree. But all I really did was stop pursuing staying ahead. And the strategy was working very well. I was in back of him by a couple of seconds and had reduced my speed and he had reduced his. It looked like everything was going to work out just perfect because I was convinced that when the time came I could drive up and pass him—he'd gone a little loose in the corners, in fact.

"So, everything was going great. But suddenly A. J. was giving me a board that Johnny Thomson, running third, and back about 15 seconds, was gaining. And pretty soon Thomson was down to 10 seconds. He was running half a second faster than Rathmann and I were, and in those days by the time it got down to 8 seconds he'd be on the same straightaway and be able to see us. And I was thinking, God, I don't want this to become a *three*-car race.

"So I decided I had to change my strategy again, and would have to re-pass Rathmann, then pray for a yellow flag or something. Three and a half laps later I was leading and going down the back straightaway when my right front came through the cord.

"But the other thing that had happened was that the moment I'd made the decision to go past Rathmann, Johnny Thomson had swallowed a valve. He was no longer a factor. But I'd committed myself and had to slow down.

"Anyway," Rodger smiled, "that's how Jim Rathmann managed to win the 500—by taking advantage of a cripple. In fact, in Victory Circle if you looked at his own right rear, it was down to the cord. It just got there after mine did."

Out on the restaurant parking lot, it was another hot and smoggy L.A. afternoon. As we were parting, I asked Rodger if he now thought that back in 1960 he'd have been better off not having had a cockpit weight jacker. And I mentioned how Jud Phillips, who never believed that race drivers had the intelligence to operate such devices anyway, once said that he always deliberately mounted his own someplace in the cockpit where they'd be sure to vibrate and break.

Rodger replied that he didn't know about any of that. Then he asked if I'd ever heard the strange story about his magneto.

"Well, you'll love this," he said. "It happened just a few months after the 1960 Indy, when Watson and I were at Syracuse with the Leader Card dirt car. I started back in the field but was in second place all ready to go on through to first when the engine began to pop and backfire. And because I didn't want to destroy it, I just pulled in.

"I thought I was losing the magneto, but back in Indianapolis after Watson had checked it out he told me, 'Rodger, I don't know. This mag checks out good. I can't believe there's anything wrong with it.'

"And he kept on checking everything, until it turned out that at Syracuse one of the injector nozzles had gotten a piece of dirt in it. I was greatly relieved that we'd solved the problem, because the Hoosier Hundred was only a few days away.

"Then Watson asked me if we should go and change the magneto anyway, and I asked him if we had a new one. It turned out that we didn't, but that Chickie Hirashima did. And of course Chickie had been Rathmann's chief mechanic in the 500. Chickie had planned to run this new magneto in the 500, then got busy and never had a chance to change it. So Watson and I agreed that if it was a brand new mag, it'd probably be a good idea for us to use it.

"We switched to Chickie's new mag and went to the Hoosier Hundred. I was leading by half a lap, there was a yellow flag and I slowed down, and the magneto gave up."

Ward shook his head. "So you think about it. If Jim Rathmann had run that mag at Indianapolis and it had failed, then Watson and I couldn't have borrowed it for the Hoosier Hundred. Which means that I would have won the Hoosier Hundred. Which means that I would have won the national points championship that year instead of being second. Which also means that I would have won the 1960 Indy 500."

Rodger grinned to show that he wasn't being serious. "You can go nuts," he concluded, "playing with things like that."

*T*he 1960 500 never would have happened the way it did had not a couple of Jim Rathmann's powerful and wealthy friends decided that the time had at long last come for Jim to win Indianapolis. He'd already been runner-up three times, and they were fed up with all that bridesmaid's business.

Social-climbing and ingratiating himself with high-toned tycoons was always part of Jim's racing life; for many of his dinosaur years he had at his disposal the richest Indy car owner baron of them all, Lindsey Hopkins. But two Texas pals of Lindsey's who took a special shine to Jim and vowed to put him in Victory Circle were Kenny Rich, the Dallas wildcat oilie, and Paul Lacey, the souped-up commodities broker. Accordingly, for 1960 Kenny and Paul wooed Jim away from Lindsey and let Jim decide his destiny by putting his own team together.

It was Rich's and Lacey's money, but Jim had full permission to tell them how to spend it. So he got them to pay A. J. Watson to build a new roadster, the Ken-Paul. Then he got them to try hiring

Larry Shinoda served as Leader Card pit-board man in 1959, here, and in 1960, when Jim Rathmann also took advantage of Larry's signals. *Indy 500 Photos*

Watson as its chief mechanic, but the Head was happy with Bob Wilke and Rodger Ward and Leader Card. Settling for what seemed like the next best thing in chiefs, Jim had Ken and Paul buy him Chickie Hirashima.

So far, so good. But around April 1960 Jim decided to spend still more money bringing in somebody who during the 500 could service him with the fastest pit stops of all. Which could only mean one man—if Jim could get him—Smokey Yunick.

Yunick was a heavyweight of stock car racing, maybe *the* heavyweight, as famous as anybody in NASCAR, including its drivers. Smokey's taxicabs regularly won the great southern marathons at Daytona and Darlington. And his rap sheet said that he was an innovator, inventor, internal combustion scientist, a bender of all the rules, and in possession of a wild temper. Formidable looking, and frequently scowling, he dressed in black stomping boots, black bad-guy hat, and a set of pristine white mechanic's coveralls whose backside blared the defiant opinion:

Smokey's
Best Damn Garage in Town
Daytona Beach, FL

The Best Damn Garage in Town was Smokey's automotive laboratory and general lair of black magic, as well as the birthplace of all the ball-buster Fords and Pontiacs that Yunick routinely treated to some of the fastest pit stops in NASCAR. But, per Smokey's account, at the beginning of 1960 he'd suffered so many business reversals that he was stone-broke, sleeping on an army cot inside The Best Damn Garage speculating that

Dinosaur roadster aesthetics took a brutal knock in 1963 when, at the last instant, Firestone put on the market lower and squatter rubber. Many teams were thrown into disorder because there weren't enough of the new wide Firestones and new fat wheels to go around. Alarmists began predicting another crash-and-burn 500 because several teams were cutting down and carving up their brake calipers and discs to make the wide Flintstones fit; supposedly this would lead to fatigue fractures and disasters. Luckily, it didn't. Roadsters, in fact, grew safer and easier to race because the wide doughnuts gave drivers additional control and confidence. The dinosaurs themselves ended up the losers, though. Those fat Flintstones knocked all their old proportions out of scale; dinosaurs never recovered their looks, never again seemed so low slung and even majestic as they had on their tall tires. Compare the J. H. Rose Trucking Special of 1962 with the doughnut rubber Agajanian Bowes Seal Fast of 1964. *Bob Tronolone*

probably he was never ever going to be solvent again. Then came that fateful call from Jim Rathmann.

Smokey: "Rathmann says, 'Hey, Smokey, I've got a brand new Watson for the 500, got all the good stuff, got a couple of car owners from Dallas, Texas, with plenty of money, got Chickie Hirashima as mechanic. Now all I need is a good chief.

"I go, 'Hell, from what I understand Chickie *is* good, as good as they get.'

"Rathmann goes, 'Yeah, but there's absolutely no way he can work the pits. He's old and his nerves are shot. I need you as co-chief.'

"So I say, 'Listen, I don't like this deal. You're telling me that this guy I don't even know says he'll be glad to work with me as co-chief. I won't touch it with a 10-foot pole. The only way I will, is if Chickie

agrees that once we roll out on race morning he don't have nothing to say about nothing.' And Rathmann says, 'That's no problem at all. Chickie doesn't even want to be in the pits on race day.'

"I said that maybe there was something to talk about after all, but that I wanted to hear about it from everybody. So I set up a conference call. Kenny Rich, Paul Lacey, Rathmann, Chickie Hirashima, and I got on a five-way hookup, and I asked Chickie, 'You sure this sounds OK to you? That we'll be co-chiefs? I don't want to get up to Indy and get into a big argument.' And Chickie said, 'Oh, hell yeah. I can help with the engines and stuff. But when it comes down to qualifying and racing the car, I can't handle that anymore.'

"I was in pretty desperate shape for money, and I asked Rathmann how much. He said ten grand, and this was when two

The Milwaukee mile, August 18, 1963, the day the dinosaur dance ended. Jimmy Clark's Lotus-powered-by-Ford leads all 200 miles and easily laps every roadster except runner-up A. J. Foyt's. *Armin Krueger*

Previous pages: Mating a four-cammer Ford to a Watson roadster, as Watson and Leader Card attempted in 1965, might have made a winner. But the thing blew up in a test and Leader Card moved down to Funny Cars. *Bob Tronolone*

hundred a week was big pay for an Indy chief. The winning chief also got a big chest of tools, a complete wardrobe, and lots of other free crap. So I said all right.

"I got up to Indy on May 1 and filled out the form as co-chief and handed it back to the registrar who asked me who was going to pay for it. I told him to charge it against car No. 4, the Ken-Paul. Then the registrar started to sign the thing but said, 'Wait a minute, Smokey. You've got co-chief here, and Chickie already signed in as chief.'

"I said, 'Just leave it the way it is for now, and we'll get it straightened out.' I went up to the garage, Paul Lacey was there, Kenny Rich was there, Jim Rathmann was there, Chickie Hirashima was there. We all shook hands and I told Rathmann, 'I went down there to sign in as co-chief and they already got Chickie signed in as chief. That isn't the deal we had at all."

"'NO PROBLEM,' says Rathmann—you know the way the sumbitch talks—'I'll go straighten it out right now.' Then he left, and I thought he had. Never even gave it a second thought."

Of course the Ken-Paul team with all its big bucks and big talent went on to win the 500, and all the wild celebrating around and in the swimming pool of the Speedway Motel had gotten followed by more celebrating at the Victory Banquet downtown. Jim Rathmann was introduced as winner and called on stage.

"Then," Smokey continued, "they were getting to the chief mechanic's part. And I've got my arms on the chair to get up because I'm next. Only it never happened. They introduced Chickie instead.

"That's when it dawned on me what had really happened, and that Rathmann had never changed the sign-in papers like he said he was going to. So I left the banquet early, pissed, and Kenny Rich later asked me how come. 'You must have been awful goddamn drunk not to notice what happened,' I told him. 'I was supposed to be co-chief on that mechanic's deal!' "

And Smokey, as it turned out, was hardly the only unhappy camper at team Ken-Paul. Also finding himself sideways with Jim Rathmann was Chickie Hirashima, who was all steamed up over Jim's post-500 remarks about the Meyer-Drake in Rodger Ward's second-place Leader Card 1 having been a vastly better engine than the Ken-Paul's, which had been a dog. Chickie, who had assembled both engines and made sure that they were equal, took Rathmann's criticism as an outrageous insult to his Meyer-Drake skills. But the 1960 500's oddest epilogue of all occurred later that summer when Jim, in a failed attempt to use Ken-Paul money to blow up Bob Wilke's Leader Card team, tried dumping Chickie *and* Smokey as mechanics and replacing them with A. J. Watson. Jim still had the hots for the Head.

The next year, very little of the original Ken-Paul group remained. Having won the only Indy 500 he'd ever seen, Paul Lacey decided that enough was enough and was out of there. Chickie Hirashima left Ken-Paul and Wilke hired him as chief of the Leader Card 41. Smokey Yunick was persona non grata, period. One of The Best Damn Garage in Town's factory Pontiacs won NASCAR's 1961 Daytona 500, and the Indy-sanctioning U.S. Auto Club had Smokey

under suspension for what it considered his crime of competing with a rival racing body.

Jim Rathmann's relentless lobbying got Smokey out of the jam and his suspension lifted in time for the 1961 Indy. Re-instated as the Ken-Paul's chief, Smokey had Jim and that great Watson, now named the Simoniz 4, running just as fast as in 1960 until another magneto quit sparking. Renumbered the Simoniz 44 for 1962, Jim raced it for the last time and demonstrated that he had lost all his attack-on-sight momentum as a dinosaur driver. Qualifying 23rd, he stroked home 9th. Returning for his retirement 500 of 1963, he was even slower, time-trialing 29th in the Coral Harbour 16 of Lindsey Hopkins, then dropping out before halfway.

Smokey, meanwhile, continued racing throughout the sixties and seventies. One of his NASCAR taxicabs scorched Daytona with stock car racing's first 3-mile-a-minute lap. And at Indy he bedeviled the Brickyard with some of the weirdest experimental iron ever seen—everything from his unsuccessful 900-horsepower turbocharged stock-block atomic bombs of the seventies to his lethal "Python" and scary "Capsule Car" of the sixties.

Out of active racing by the eighties, Smokey metamorphosed into one of the world's most conspicuous automotive authorities, he and his black hats serving variously as good will ambassadors and PR mouthpieces to the Big Three in Detroit and Dearborn, plus Smokey taking pen in hand as a highly opinionated magazine columnist and all-around colorful personality.

Despite all this, as the years passed Smokey developed—somewhat in the ax-grinding manner of Herb Porter and Frank Kurtis—a fixation that roadster Indianapolis had ill-treated him, and that what had happened at the 1960 Victory Banquet should be reversed and credit for being Indy's winning chief mechanic, or even its co-winning chief, should be granted him.

The Best Damn Garage in Town in Daytona Beach being not that far from Jim Rathmann Cadillac in Melbourne, Smokey at one point apparently approached Jim to get Jim to agree that, yes, Smokey did merit co-chief mechanic's credit with Chickie Hirashima; but Jim, for whatever reason, would not. So the friendship hit the wall. Their dispute might easily have been resolved elsewhere, but in the small and closed dinosaur world it went on festering for years.

Among the many whom Smokey has since turned to plead his case, so far unsuccessfully, has been Kenny Rich. "Absolutely the most important element of the 1960 Ken-Paul team was Smokey Yunick," Kenny told me in a phone conversation. "I even wrote a letter to Dick King, the president of the U.S. Auto Club, saying that as far as I was concerned the Indianapolis records should be changed, and that Smokey deserves getting credit with Chickie as co-chief. Smokey was instrumental. Chickie couldn't have won the 500 without Smokey. There's absolutely no way. And I think what proves it is that in 1961 when we had the choice of going with Chickie or Smokey, we went with Smokey." But apparently the U.S. Auto Club still wouldn't agree to change the records.

Taking another hard whack at roadsters' graceful good looks were all the various and variously ugly ram-air hood devices triggered by the Meyer-Drake Offenhauser's sudden demand for more oxygen in the face of the threat of the four-cam Ford. The nice looking Racing Associates 46 of 1963 *(opposite page, top)* ended up in 1964 the hulking Bardahl 86 *(above and opposite page, bottom)* which barely survived the second lap's monster crash and fire. *Bob Tronolone, Indy 500 Photos*

And the animosity between Smokey and Jim expanded. When the restored version of the Ken-Paul went on display at the Hall of Fame with "Driver: Jim Rathmann" on its flanks, one of Smokey's old pals within the museum had contrived to add "Mechanic: Smokey Yunick". But Smokey's name subsequently got painted over, and when he learned the erasure had been done at the personal behest of Jim Rathmann, Smokey took his own revenge of sorts. If you ever happened to be in Daytona visiting The Best Damn Garage in Town and had to go see a man about a horse, Jim Rathmann's face would be smiling up at you from a photograph pasted on the toilet bowl.

"*I* don't know how you guys get this thing so screwed up!" Smokey barked at me one morning in May 1995 over breakfast at Charlie Brown's restaurant out on High School Road near the Speedway. And things got worse after that.

Probably what I should have mentioned earlier was that Smokey and I were friends until I started monkeying around with the Ken-Paul controversy. We were co-workers. During the eighties both of us were writing for the same racing magazine, and every May we'd see one another at Indianapolis. I always looked forward to strolling through Gasoline Alley and the racing pits while we checked out the scene and Smokey gossiped with longtime dinosaur buddies, signed autographs, and rated the Hoosier femme scenery. He hasn't really come across that way here, but Smokey, in addition to being one of racing's great movers and shakers of the last five decades, can also be a very funny man. I loved listening to him talk.

And talk Smokey would, about almost everything, but especially about (1) his early life in stock car racing as its premier rogue mechanic and witty builder, deviously playing the NASCAR rule book five ways against the middle; and (2) the Offy roadster era of Gasoline Alley days and White Front nights. But Smokey was a great man for carrying a grudge, and I quickly learned that merely mentioning Jim Rathmann's name could set off an explosion. And after I involved myself in sorting out the Ken-Paul chief mechanic situation, I discovered that mentioning Chickie Hirashima was another unwise risk: "Chickie was never in the pits during the 1960 500! I did the whole goddamn thing!"

Who was I to argue? I hadn't even been there. And Chickie, dead of stomach cancer since Christmas Day 1980, could scarcely rebut or confirm what Smokey was saying. It sounds like Rathmann made the same promise—that he would be crew chief—to both Chickie and Smokey, but he talked to Chickie first and Chickie never knew he'd made the same promise to Smokey. In fact I don't believe that Chickie had been aware that Smokey ever had a beef at all, and I say that because I once wrote a magazine article about Chickie while he was still alive, and Chickie never mentioned a thing about it. And he'd said nothing about being such a decrepit nervous wreck that he no longer could hack the challenge of the 500.

Candidly, I had a hard time swallowing that one myself. If Chickie in 1960 had been physically unable to work in the pits, how come he'd next served as pit chief of the Leader Card 41/Leader Card 7 in 1961 and 1962? The latter year I'd personally watched Chickie and the Leader Card 7's driver Len Sutton energetically jumping up and down for joy at being the 500's runners-up.

But I didn't want to go into that with Smokey; he'd dispute it, either saying that I'd misquoted Chickie or that my own memory must be slipping. Quite possibly it was. But then, fortunately, I discovered a glossy photograph of the 1960 500 that I was certain settled the issue of whether or not Chickie had been in the pits. It showed a rubber and refueling stop in progress. Both front wheels of the Ken-Paul were off, and the tire gang was scrambling while Smokey dumped fuel and a lone fireman stood by with the usual pop-gun extinguisher. And while all this was going on, Chickie, dressed in a fancy Ken-Paul uniform like everybody else, was reaching over the pit wall with a long stick passing a fresh set of goggles to Jim Rathmann in the Ken-Paul's cockpit.

Even though the photograph only showed his back, it was unmistakably Chickie, or at least it certainly was to me. And I was sure that Smokey would feel the same way when I showed it to him during our fateful oatmeal breakfast at Charlie Brown's. The restaurant is a noisy and happy place during May, and on this particular morning, as ever, was filled with race people, many of whom were stopping by our table to tell Smokey hello. The effects of all that blasting horsepower roaring through his ears for half a century has taken the edge off Smokey's hearing anyway, so I had to raise my voice to be heard.

"Smokey," I began, tentatively, after he'd finished his oatmeal, "if I show you a picture of something that contradicts what you've been saying about Chickie . . ."

"Yeah?"

"Well, I just want to show you something." And I handed him the glossy of the pit stop.

"This is 1960," I went on. "You're refueling, and Rathmann is getting new goggles from Chickie."

"Who?"

"That's Chickie giving the goggles on the stick."

Smokey looked at the photo again. "That's Chickie?"

"Yes."

"How do you know?"

"It's him," I said. Then I decided to try something else. "Listen, I don't want to steam you, I just . . ."

"Well, how do you know that's Chickie?"

"Because you can recognize him."

"He wasn't in the pits."

This was going to be more difficult than I'd thought.

"I know that's what you say, but . . ."

"If that's a picture of Chickie, it's not a race day picture. Maybe it's a practice pit stop on Carburetion Day. Chickie wasn't there on race day."

"You'll still put your life on that?"

In 1965, the Weinberger Homes became the last front-engine at Indy to complete all 200 laps, in fifth position. For the privilege of being able to lock into serious combat with flyweight funny cars, it had had to surrender whatever pounds it could. Much of its handsome coachwork got junked and only a naked fuel bladder served as its tail. In 1967, at Phoenix International Raceway in its very last championship start, two funny cars ganged up on it in a crash. And it knocked the crap out of both of them. *Bob Tronolone*

"Well, hell yeah!"

Things were getting mean. I knew I was beaten, wishing I'd never showed him the damn picture at all.

"I guarantee when you get a real race day picture of Chickie in the pits, he's going to have his street clothes on."

Was it worth telling Smokey that there are Victory Circle photographs of Chickie being the first to greet Jim in the Ken-Paul, laying three slobbery wet kisses on him—Jim looks startled—and that Chickie is wearing the Ken-Paul colors? I doubted it. Smokey would just say that Chickie must have changed into his Ken-Paul uniform for the Victory Circle cameras.

It really was time to go. The breakfast had been a disaster. Worse, I could sense that Smokey and I would never again be on the same good terms. So could Smokey.

"I hope I helped you," he said as we parted, his tone signifying just the opposite. "And if I didn't, tough shit."

Smokey had handled the Ken-Paul's refueling duties in the 1960 500, and I went looking around for the other members of the old pit crew. Serving as left front wheel changer and also working as the jack man who hit the air hose, had been the dinosaur driver Al Keller, aka the Dirty Indian. On the left rear had been Bruce Crower, the Offenhauser specialist and grinder of hot camshafts, and on the right rear had been Bob Bubenik, A. J. Foyt's brother-in-law, another respected citizen of Gasoline Alley. The three of them were a typical pickup gang organized at the last moment after their own entry that year—a pushrod stock-block oddity sponsored by a group of house builders from Chula Vista, California—had missed the show. The fourth Ken-Paul crew member had been Ronnie Kaplan. Normally a chief mechanic himself, he'd volunteered for duty after the Lesovsky lowbelly laydown he'd been assigned to had flopped.

The Dirty Indian had gotten killed at Phoenix in a dirt track crash a year afterward, and for one reason or another I could never make contact with Bruce Crower. But I managed to speak by telephone to Ronnie Kaplan in Chicago and to Bob Bubenik in Houston.

"I'd never previously worked on an Indy car team where a race driver called all the shots instead of its car owners or its chief mechanic," Ronnie remembered. "So it surprised me to see Jim Rathmann doing that at Ken-Paul. And it surprised me to see Smokey Yunick working in the capacity of mechanic when ordinarily he would have been a chief. Jim and I were old friends from Chicago racing, and Smokey and I from stock cars down south. Chickie Hirashima and I had known each other from every 500 since 1953.

"What I remember about the race was that Jim and Rodger Ward were so closely matched on the racetrack that they couldn't escape each other. When Jim would jump ahead of Ward, all of us were jumping up and down and elated. And when Ward passed him back we were yelling at Jim to go get 'em, go get 'em. All our pit stops were maximum pressure green flag stops. What was frustrating was that no matter how fast they were, A. J. Watson and the rest of Ward's bunch at Leader Card, who were just a few stalls up from us, always matched us. All of us were thinking, 'Let's get this race won!' "

Bob Bubenik remembered, "Smokey was managing our pit stops, and he had all that good experience from NASCAR. I was looking after the right rear and everyone on the crew was coordinated and looking after each other. But what really focused us, I think, was late in the 500 when Chickie jumped up and said, 'Hey, we're gonna win this thing!' He just knew it in his mind. And then we all began to pay even more attention."

I asked Bob if he'd been aware of any tension at Ken-Paul between Smokey and Chickie.

"I came to the team so late, it was hard to say what the general feeling was," he replied. "Smokey and Chickie didn't seem to speak to each other a lot, but Chickie was always a quiet little guy anyway. And Smokey was the other way around. He talked a lot in those days."

"He talks a lot now," I agreed.

"The whole thing has become twisted out of shape," Bob said. "So many people think that they were the cause of greatness. And none of us need to lay claim to that. We just need to think of all the great times we had. Forget the bad times, remember the good ones."

To get the news from the Ken-Paul's opposition, I'd spoken to Larry Shinoda. In that 1960 500, as ever, he'd performed the Leader Card pit board signals to Rodger Ward.

"Ward should have won the 500," Larry said. "He had his right front breaker cord go the same time as Rathmann's right rear did, but the difference was that Ward could see his and automatically slowed down. But Rathmann couldn't see his, and that was why he kept standing on it without knowing any better.

"Of course Rathmann always goes crazy whenever I tell him that; he insists he blew off Ward fair and square. And Rathmann's own pit board man was another old friend of mine, a ratchetjaw named Bill Yeager. He still gets all pissed off at me for something else that happened that year. I was signaling Ward with a custom-made board with extra-bright Velcro numbers, and Yeager was signaling Rathmann with an old junk blackboard that Rathmann couldn't read. So every lap Rathmann was ignoring Yeager's signals and instead reading and stealing mine to Ward. I still like to strap that on Yeager, until finally Yeager goes, 'Fuck your signals. We won.'

"The guy who really should have won was Johnny Thomson in Herb Porter's and Rocky Philipp's laydown. That was a fast car. It had both Rathmann and Ward beat, blown away. Only it broke."

*P*ositive, I must be positive.

Who knows? Maybe it's only fitting and appropriate that the pair of Watsons who fought the outstanding roadster match should wind up morphed into the same automobile sitting and sharing the same space in the Speedway Hall of Fame.

So let's leave it at that, and I will gratefully back out of the disputatious yarn of the Ken-Paul and the Leader Card 1 with one of the most upbeat quotations I know of.

"I loved all the roadsters," one of the great journeyman dinosaur drivers once told me. And he added "All of them made my hair stand on end."

He's a geezer guy now, all of us are geezer guys now, and as bald as a worn-out Flintstone. Timeless sentiments, though. Watching the Offy roadsters of the Indy 500 always made the hair stand up on the back of my neck too. What great race cars those big suckers were.

INDEX